HAROUN AND THE SEA OF STORIES

Salman Rushdie

AUTHORED by Lane Davis
UPDATED AND REVISED by Bella Wang

COVER DESIGN by Table XI Partners LLC
COVER PHOTO by Olivia Verma and © 2005 GradeSaver, LLC

BOOK DESIGN by Table XI Partners LLC

Published by GradeSaver LLC, www.gradesaver.com

First published in the United States of America by GradeSaver LLC. 2011

GRADESAVER, the GradeSaver logo and the phrase "Getting you the grade since 1999" are registered trademarks of GradeSaver, LLC

ISBN 978-1-60259-250-6

Printed in the United States of America

For other products and additional information please visit
http://www.gradesaver.com

Table of Contents

Biography of Rushdie, Salman (1947-)..1

About Haroun and the Sea of Stories..3

Character List..5

Major Themes..7

Glossary of Terms..9

Short Summary...11

Quotes and Analysis..15

Summary and Analysis of Chapters 1-2..19

Summary and Analysis of Chapters 3-4..23

Summary and Analysis of Chapters 5-6..27

Summary and Analysis of Chapters 7-8..31

Summary and Analysis of Chapters 9-10..35

Summary and Analysis of Chapters 11-12...39

Suggested Essay Questions..43

The Source Stories..47

Author of ClassicNote and Sources...49

Essay: Haroun's Multicolored Backdrop..51

Quiz 1...55

Quiz 1 Answer Key..61

Quiz 2...63

Quiz 2 Answer Key..69

Table of Contents

Quiz 3..71

Quiz 3 Answer Key...77

Quiz 4..79

Quiz 4 Answer Key...85

Biography of Rushdie, Salman (1947-)

Salman Rushdie is one of the leading Anglo-Indian novelists of the twentieth century, taking inspiration from a variety of genres in his writing. His style is often likened to magic realism, which mixes religion, fantasy, and mythology into reality. He has been compared to authors such as Peter Carey, Emma Tennant, and Angela Carter. The familiar way in which some of his works treat religion has provoked criticism, however, peaking in the Ayatollah of Iran issuing death threats in response to *The Satanic Verses*, his fourth novel.

Ahmed Salman Rushdie was born on June 19, 1947 in Bombay, India to a middle class Muslim family. His father was a businessman, educated in Cambridge, and his grandfather was an Urdu poet. At fourteen, he was sent to England for schooling, attending the Rugby School in Warwickshire. In 1964, his family, responding to the growing hostilities between India and Pakistan, joined many emigrating Muslims and moved to Karachi, Pakistan.

The religious and political conflicts of his homeland affected Rushdie deeply, although he stayed in England to attend the King's College in Cambridge and studying history. While in school, he also joined the Cambridge Footlights theatre company. Following graduation, in 1968 he began working in Pakistani television. Later, he also acted in the Oval House theatre group in Kennington, England, and until 1981, he wrote freelance copy for advertisers Ofilvy and Mather and Charles Barker.

In 1975, Rushdie published his first novel. *Grimus*, a science fiction story inspired by the twelfth century Sufi poem "The Conference of the Birds," was largely ignored by both critics and the public. Rushdie's literary fortunes changed in 1981. The publication of his second novel *Midnight's Children* brought him international fame and acclaim. The story is a comic allegory of Indian history, and involves the 1001 children born after India's Declaration of Independence, each of whom possesses a magical power. It won the Booker Prize for Fiction, the English-Speaking Union Award, the James Tait Black Memorial Prize (fiction), an Arts Council Writers' Award, and in 1993 and 2008, was named the "Booker of Bookers," acknowledging it as the best recipient of the Booker Prize for Fiction in the award's history.

His third novel, [Shame] (1983), was commonly regarded as a political allegory of Pakistani politics, using a wealthy family as a metaphor for the country and basing two of its characters on former Prime Minister Zulfikar Ali Bhutto and General Muhammad Zia-ul-Haq. It won the Prix du Meilleur Livre Etranger and made the short list for the Booker Prize. In 1987, he published a short travel narrative titled *The Jaguar's Smile*.

In 1988, Rushdie became the center of a controversy surrounding the publication of his fourth novel, *The Satanic Verses*, which revolves around two Indian actors who struggle with religion, spirituality, and nationality. Although the book won the Whitbread Award, Rushdie's free use of Islamic history and theology caused the orthodox Muslim Ayatollah Khomeini of Iran to issue of a fatwa, a call to all obedient Muslims to assassinate him. The book was banned and burned in many countries, and several people involved with its publication were injured and killed. After the death threat, Rushdie shunned publicity and went into hiding for many years, although he continued to write.

He published a book of children's stories in 1990 titled *Haroun and the Sea of Stories* which won the Writers' Guild Award (Best Children's Book), followed by a collection of essays, *Imaginary Homelands: Essays and Criticism 1981-1991* (1991), and a collection of short stories, *East, West* (1994). Then came another novel, *The Moor's Last Sigh* (1995), which used a family's history to explore the activities of right-wing Hindu terrorists and the cultural connections between India and the Iberian peninsula. *The Ground Beneath Her Feet* (1999) was Rushdie's sixth novel, re-imagining the birth of modern rock music. He also published the novel *Fury* in 2001 and *Step Across This Line: Collected Non-fiction 1992-2002* in 2002. His latest work is the novel *Shalimar the Clown*, published in 2005 and a finalist for the Whitbread Book Awards.

Rushdie ended his fourth marriage to the American television star Padma Lakshmi in 2007. He is Honorary Professor in the Humanities at the Massachusetts Institute of Technology, Distinguished Supporter of the British Humanist Association, Distinguished Fellow in Literature at the University of Anglia, recipient of the 1993 Austrian State Prize for European Literature, recipient of the 1996 Aristeion Literary Prize, and Fellow of the Royal Society of Literature and *Commandeur de Arts et des Lettres*. He was also President of PEN American Center from 2003-2005. In 2000, he moved from London to New York. In 2006, he became the Distinguished Writer in Residence at Emory University in Atlanta, Georgia.

About Haroun and the Sea of Stories

Salmon Rushdie first began orally composing the stories that comprise *Haroun and the Sea of Stories* while writing his famous novel *The Satanic Verses*. During this time, Rushdie's nine-year-old son, Zafar, chastised his father for not writing books that children could read. Rushdie made a deal with his son that the next novel he wrote would be for children.

Rushdie began comprising the stories in the book by telling them to his son during bath time. According to Rushdie, "I would have these basic motifs, like the Sea of Stories, but each time I would improvise--not only to please him but to test myself, to see if I could just say something and take it elsewhere." By beginning the novel's stories in oral form, Rushdie mirrors the challenge of the character of Rashid: how to create meaningful stories in a world that does not value fantasy.

In terms of genre, Rushdie wrote the novel as something that children would enjoy but that adults would understand. The surface tension of the novel is the relationship between a father and a son, yet the deeper meaning of the novel centers on the meaning of stories and storytelling. It incorporates many of the themes of Rushdie's other works; magic realism, identity, and politics, amongst others.

Critics have also read *Haroun* in terms of the personal and political struggles that Rushdie experienced during the *fatwa* issued against him by the leader of Iran, the Ayatollah Ruhollah Khomeini for his novel *The Satanic Verses*. The *fatwa* called for Rushdie's death and death to those that facilitated the book's publication for its depictions of Islam and Muslims. *Haroun*, which was partially written while the controversy was going on, playfully deals with the reality of violence directed against Rushdie for his fictional work by engaging the idea of silence and the power of storytelling.

Rushdie did not mean for the book to be a *serious* allegory, however. His perception of the work is that it must be read as a playful work of fiction. Rushdie explained the book as primary a work of story: "Haroun is a tale. Even to call it a parable is too much. It must have, as they say, no designs upon it. Zafar will not read it to advance the public good, or even to comfort his father. He must read it for fun."

About Haroun and the Sea of Stories

Character List

Haroun

Haroun is the hero of the story. He is a boy that travels to Kahani to help restore his father's storytelling power.

Rashid

Rashid is Haroun's father. He is a master storyteller that loses his ability to tell stories after his wife leaves him.

Iff the Water Genie

Iff is a Water Genie responsible for care of the Story Water that comes from the moon Kahani. He accompanies Haroun on his journey.

Mali

Mali is a Water Gardener. He cares for the story streams in the Sea of Stories on Kahani.

Butt the Hoopoe

Butt the Hoopoe is a mechanical bird that flies Haroun to the moon Kahani and accompanies him on his journey.

Goopy

Goopy is a Plentimaw fish that helps Haroun as he ventures to the land of Chup.

Bagha

Bagha is a Plentimaw fish that accompanies Haroun. The Plentimaw fish are so named because they talk in rhyme all the time.

Prince Bolo

Bolo is the prince of the land of Gup. He leads the Guppee army to Chup in order to rescue his princess fiance Batcheat.

Princess Batcheat

Batcheat is princess of the land of Gup. She is captured by Khattam-Shud and the forces of Chup.

Khattam-Shud

Khattam-Shud, which means "silence," is the novel's antagonist. He poisons the story streams of the Sea of Stories and captures Princess Batcheat.

Mudra the Shadow Warrior

Mudra is a former Chupwala soldier. He leaves the army because he disagrees with Khattam-Shud and helps the Guppees in their fight against the Chupwala army.

Blabbermouth

Blabbermouth is a Page in the Library (army) of Gup. She disguises herself as a boy but is found out after she saves the Guppee leadership from a suicide bomber.

General Kitab

General Kitab is the general for the Guppee army. He is known for talking openly and freely about his battle plans.

The Walrus

The Walrus is the head of the P2C2E (Processes 2 Complicated 2 Explain) on Kahani. He is the person Haroun is trying to talk to in order to get his father's Story Water turned on again.

Butt the Mail Coach Driver

Butt the Mail Coach Driver drives Haroun and Rashid to the Valley of K. He is known for his alliteration of speech and his reckless driving.

Snooty Buttoo

Snooty Buttoo is an autocrat politician in the Valley of K. He brings in Rashid to tell stories to help him be elected.

Mrs. Oneeta Sengupta

Mrs. Sengupta lives above Haroun's family in the sad city. Her husband runs off with Haroun's mother.

Mr. Sengupta

Mr. Sengupta is a measly man who lives above the Khalifa family in the sad city. He has no appreciation for story and steals Haroun's mother away from the family.

Major Themes

The Importance of Story

The conflict that begins the action of the novel revolves around the importance of stories in a person's life. Both of the people that Rashid Khalifa loves, his son and his wife, both turn on him and tell him that his stories are not real and do not matter. Without his stories, Rashid finds that he has no way to support himself or to justify his life. Haroun's quest is not just an adventure to return Rashid's stories to him, but it is also a son's journey to give meaning to his father's life. In this way, Rushdie suggests that a person's stories compose their identity and dignity.

Censorship

The idea of censorship is a sustained motif in the novel. This is largely a reflection on Rushdie's own experience of censorship when the Ayatollah placed a fatwa upon him for his depiction of Islam in The Satanic Verses. Chupwala and its dictator Khattam-Shud represent this censorship. Khattam-Shud wishes not only to poison the Sea of Stories, but he also wishes to silence the stories completely. Chup, therefore, is not only a land of darkness, but also a land of complete silence and censorship. The Land of Gup, on the other hand, is a land of complete Freedom of Speech, even to those that would criticize the land's leaders in what might be considered anarchy. On the surface, Rushdie would seem to favor the Guppees' freedom over the strict authoritarian censorship of the Chupwala's, though later passages in the novel blur these lines of distinction.

The Balance between Silence and Speech

A cursory reading would seem to suggest that Rushdie favors the Land of Gup and the light that creates its ever present stories and freedom of speech. However, Rushdie indicates that both Gup and Chup are two sides of a whole. Each must exist in balance with the other to create a median existence. This is evident in the Guppees' own contradictory behavior; though they favor complete freedom, their own Eggheads at P2C2E House create an imbalance in light that leaves the Chupwalas in perpetual darkness against their will. This suggests that all societies have some propensity to censor others. Likewise, the Guppees risk defeat and incompetence from their inability to censor their criticisms and gossip. This speech is unproductive speech. Though Rushdie clearly opposes censorship, his novel deftly explores the balance needed in a society between the control and expression of speech.

The Playfulness of Language

Rushdie originally wrote *Haroun and the Sea of Stories* for his children. As a young adult novel, Rushdie creates the strange alternate world of Kahani through a strange and playful use of language. Characters in the novel embody literary devices such as alliteration, rhyme, and orality. The rhythms and eccentricities of the language represent that particular character and illuminates their particular traits. On another level, Rushdie is also commenting on the elusiveness of language. He creates words and phrases to highlight the fact that the reader can never quite grasp the true meaning of a text or an author's intention. The reader is confounded by the language and patterns of usage so that the moon of Kahani feels foreign.

The Foolishness of War

The final battle between the Guppees and the Chupwala's is Rushdie's commentary on war fought for political, religious, or personal reasons. Rushdie creates two armies that go to war for foolish reasons: their inability to communicate. This war makes them literally look foolish. In order to protect their noses from freezing over, each soldier puts on a small nose-warmer that looks like a clown nose. The armies look like clowns as they fight. This is an embodiment of the idiocy of their war. The foolishness comes to light when it is learned that the Chupwalas fight only because they are afraid not to do so. This war, therefore, has nothing to do with bravery, courage, or honor.

Control through Language

The Cultmaster Khattam-Shud tells Haroun that the world is not made for Fun but is, instead, made for controlling. The way that the Cultmaster attempts to assert this control is by controlling the way people speak. He has gained control over the Chupwalas by polluting the stories they tell and the language they use. Without a use for language, the people become silent and are then able to be controlled. This is a commentary on authoritarian regimes, especially in the Middle East, that silence their people through political, social, and religious means. Without the tradition of story, people lose their freedom.

The Beauty of Darkness

In a brief passage, Haroun watches Mudra the Shadow Warrior in a martial dance with his shadow. This dance shows Haroun that darkness, and the evil that Haroun believes it represents, is not always meant to oppose light or goodness even if it is its opposite. In this sense, darkness and light do not cancel each other out but, instead, complement each other. Night becomes as valuable as day, and darkness contains its own intrinsic value. What represents true evil in the novel is the hatred that Khattam-Shud has towards the Land of Gup and the Stories of the Sea.

Glossary of Terms

Abhinaya

Abhinaya is the Language of Gesture used by Mudra the Shadow Warrior.

Alifbay

Alifbay is the land in which Haroun and his family live. It is a name composed of the first and last letters of the Hindustani alphabet.

Anti-climax

An anti-climax is a decline viewed in disappointing contrast with a previous rise.

aubergine

An aubergine is another name for an eggplant.

autocrat

An autocrat is a person that has unlimited power over a population of people.

Bezaban

Bezaban is an idol erected by Khattam-Shud in an attempt to worship complete silence and darkness.

cauldron

A cauldron is a large iron pot used to boil liquids.

Comptroller

A comptroller is a management level position responsible for supervising the quality of work of an organization.

Court-Martial

A court-martial is a military trial held for those accused of disobeying orders.

cultmaster

A cultmaster is the leader of a religious group of fanatics.

Franj

Franj is an ancient, dead language in the land of Alifbay.

Goodwife

A medieval term of respect for a man's spouse.

Hoopoe

The is a colourful bird that is found across Afro-Eurasia, notable for its distinctive 'crown' of feathers.

insomnia

Insomnia is a state in which a person is unable to sleep.

maw

Maw is a shorthand way of referring to incessant talking.

monkey wrench

A monkey wrench is a type of tool used especially for repairing pipes.

mutiny

Mutiny is a conspiracy among members of a military to overthrow their leaders.

P2C2E

P2C2E is the Kahani shorthand way of referring to a "Process 2 Complicated 2 Explain."

Plentimaw

Plentimaws are a type of fish in the Sea of Stories; they are named so because they talk so much.

tyres

"Tyre" is the English spelling of the word tire; the wheels of a car or vehicle.

Wishwater

Wishwater is a kind of water found in the Sea of Stories that makes anyone's wish come true.

Short Summary

The novel opens in the sad city in the country of Alifbay, where Haroun Khalifa lives with his father, a famous storyteller, and his mother. One day, Haroun arrives home from school to learn that his mother has run off with his upstairs neighbor. This neighbor had often been critical of Haroun's father, Rashid, because he did not understand the usefulness of stories. In anger, Haroun assails his father for the uselessness of his stories. This crushes his father. Haroun finds it difficult to concentrate on schoolwork and so his father decides to take him on a storytelling job he is performing for some politicos in the Land of G and the Valley of K. When Rashid attempts to tell his stories, however, no words come out, and the politicos get very mad.

Haroun and Rashid board a mail bus bound for the Valley of K. It is driven by a parrot-looking man named Butt who stutters and speaks in riddles. Rashid makes a deal with Butt to drive them on the dangerous road between the Land of G and the Valley of K. Butt drives dangerously and Haroun is worried that he will die. When they reach the beautiful sights of the Valley of K, Rashid tells Haroun that it all reminds him of "khattam-shud," an ancient concept that means silence. When they reach K, Haroun and Rashid meet Mr. Buttoo, the politician, who takes them to his boat on the Dull Lake. As they depart on the lake, they are engulfed in a thick mist.

The mist smells very bad and Haroun realizes that it is a Mist of Misery brought on by his father's foul mood. When the sea begins to rock, Haroun tells everyone to think good thoughts, and when they do, the sea calms. Haroun and Rashid reach the yacht that will take them to their destination the next day. The yacht is very luxurious, but both Rashid and Haroun have difficulty sleeping. Just as Haroun dozes off, he hears a noise in his bedroom. He finds an old man with an onion shaped head, who disappears as soon as he sees Haroun. The old man drops a wrench, which Haroun confiscates. The old man materializes and tells Haroun he is Iff, the Water Genie, and he must have the wrench to turn off the Story Stream for his father, Rashid. When Haroun protests, Iff tells him to take it up with the Walrus in Gup City, Kahani. Haroun demands that the Water Genie take him there, and Iff reluctantly concedes in order to get his wrench back from Haroun.

The Genie tells Haroun to pick a bird and give it a name and it will materialize. He pulls out a handful of tiny magical creatures. Haroun picks the Hoopoe and Iff throws it out the window and into the water where it balloons into a huge bird. They climb on its back and accelerate into space. The Hoopoe looks like Mr. Butt, so Haroun names it Butt the Hoopoe. They are able to communicate telepathically. Butt the Hoopoe lands on the Sea of Stories of Kahani, Earth's second moon, which moves so fast it is undetectable by human instruments. it evenly distributes Story Water across the earth. They land in the ocean so that Iff can give Haroun Wishwater and hopefully bypass meeting the Walrus.

Haroun drinks the Wishwater and wishes for his father's storytelling to return. He can only focus on an image of his mother, however, and after eleven minutes, he loses his concentration. Iff then gives Haroun a cup of water from the Sea that contains a story. Haroun drinks it and then finds himself looking through the eyes of a hero in a Princess Rescue story. As the hero climbs the tower to rescue the princess, he turns into a spider and princess hacks away at him until he falls to the ground. When Haroun wakes from his story, Iff tells him that someone named Khattam-Shud is poisoning the stories.

Haroun, Butt the Hoopoe, and Iff the Water Genie fly to the Land of Gup, where they meet Mali, the Water Gardner, and the Plentimaw fishes. The entire land is preparing for war. The Chupwalas have stolen Princess Batcheat from Gup. In addition, they have polluted the Sea of Stories so that many do not make sense anymore. Prince Bolo, General Kitab, and the Walrus announce their plans for war to the Pages of the Guppee Library (or, army). They bring in a spy with a hood over his head. When the hood is removed, Haroun sees his father.

Rashid tells everyone that he transported to Kahani and was in the twilight strip when he sas the Princess Batcheat captured. The Chupwalas have come under the spell of Cultmaster Khattam-Shud who wants to sacrifice her to Bezaban, an idol to silence. Prince Bolo and General Kitab declare war on Chup and Rashid offers to guide them to the Chupwala encampment. One of the soldiers in the army, Blabbermouth, takes Haroun to his room. They become lost and Haroun knocks the hat off Blabbermouth's head. Long hair falls out and Haroun sees Blabbermouth is a girl. She then entertains him with a juggling act.

The army sails towards Chup, chattering about the causes for the war in a way that Haroun thinks might be mutinous. They enter the land of Darkness and land on the beach. They explore the interior and come upon a dark warrior fighting his own shadow in a kind of seductive dance. The man realizes he is being watched and comes to find the trespassers. The shadow begins to speak. It croaks out unintelligible words until Rashid realizes the warrior is speaking in an ancient gesture language. Rashid interprets the warrior's talk. His name is Mudra and he had been second in command in Chup. He is now fighting against Khattam-Shud in order to bring peace back to Chup. Mudra agrees to help the Guppees defeat Khattam-Shud.

Haroun volunteers to spy for the army because of his love of stories. He, Iff, Butt the Hoopoe, Mali, and the Plentimaw fishes begin to trek towards the Old Zone. The water becomes so poisonous that the fish cannot go on. The remaining crew is suddenly ambushed and captured in nets. They are taken to a giant, black ship. On the deck are cauldrons of poison. To Haroun, it looks like everything is impermanent, like a shadow. Khattam-Shud appears and he is a tiny, weasly, measly man. Haroun realizes that this is Khattam-Shud's shadow that has detached from its owner. The Cultmaster tells them that stories are inefficient and useless and that is why they are being destroyed.

The ship's hull is full of darkness and machines To Complicated to Describe. The Cultmaster shows them where they are building a great Plug to seal the Story Source at the bottom of the Sea. Haroun sees roots growing through a port window and Mali appears, latching onto the generators and breaking the machines. Haroun breaks free, puts on a protective wetsuit, and dives down into the Sea where he sees the Plug being constructed. He returns to Butt the Hoopoe and takes out a vial of Wishwater given to him by Iff. He drinks it and wishes that the axis of Kahani would spin normally. A few minutes pass and then the entire land is bathed in sunlight. All of the shadows on the ship begin to fade away and soon everyone is free and the poison is destroyed.

In Chup, Khattam-Shud sends an ambassador to the Guppee army. The ambassador begins to juggle and pulls out a bomb. Only Blabbermouth's quick action keeps everyone from being blown up, but it is revealed that Blabbermouth is a girl in the process. Bolo tries to fire her, but Mudra asks her to be a part of his army because of her bravery. The battle between the army commences. Because the Guppees have had such open and honest communication, they fight as a team. The Chupwalas, because of their silence, distrust each other. The Guppee army overwhelms the Chupwala army. As the battle ends, there is a great earthquake and the moon begins to spin. The statue of Bezaban falls and crushes the real Khattam-Shud. Peace is declared and everyone receives a promotion within their rank. Haroun prepares to leave and is told that he must see the Walrus.

In the Walrus's office, Haroun learns that it is all a joke and that he is not in trouble. All his friends are there with him. The Walrus tells him that for his bravery he is to be given a happy ending to his story. Haroun doubts that this is possible, but he wishes for his city to no longer be sad. He wakes up back in the Valley of K where his father is preparing his political story. As he stands up to give it, his father tells the story of *Haroun and the Sea of Stories*. It is a story that the crowd loves and they turn against their autocratic leader, Mr. Buttoo.

When Rashid and Haroun return home, it is raining and they walk through it getting soaked. All of the people in the sad city are dancing and Haroun asks why. They claim that the city has remembered it's name, Kahani, which means "story." Haroun realizes that the Walrus has put a happy ending into the raindrops. When he arrives home, he finds his mother there, telling them that she made a mistake in running off with Mr. Sengupta. The next day, Haroun awakes to find it is his birthday and his mother singing in another room in the house.

Quotes and Analysis

"What's the use of stories that aren't even true?"

Haroun and the Sea of Stories, 22

This quote frames the central crisis of the novel: what role does story play in culture and society and what happens when it no longer has power. While the book is written for young adults, the theme of story is nuanced and complicated. Rushdie presents a land in which story is being destroyed, a symbol for the way that narrative is often destroyed in the quest for power. Haroun's journey through the novel is an answer to the question of the importance of story. The ultimate answer is that story gives meaning.

"...in the Land of Chup, a Shadow very often has a stronger personality than the Person, or Self, or Substance to whom or to which it is joined! So often the Shadow leads, and it is the Person or Self or Substance that follows. And of course there can be quarrels between the Shadow and the Substance or Self or Person; they can pull in opposite directions...but just as often there is a true partnership, and mutual respect."

Haroun and the Sea of Stories, 132

This quote is spoken by Mudra, the Shadow Warrior, in an attempt to explain the unrest and evil in the Land of Chup. The shadow and the self are meant to represent two sides of a coin: the self symbolizes the personhood and autonomy of the individual. The shadow represents the forces of culture and society, such as politics or religion, with which the self is engaged. Rushdie proposes that these two sides can often conflict with each other, such as when religion causes a person to undertake unjust acts. However, there is beauty in these social and cultural forces when they work towards the freedom of the self.

"To give a thing a name, a label, a handle; to rescue it from anonymity, to pluck it out of the Place of Namelessness, in short to identify it -- well, that's a way of bringing the said thing into being."

Haroun and the Sea of Stories, 63

This quote is spoken by Iff the Water Genie as he tries to explain to Haroun the power and reason behind the fantastical and magical events happening to him. This quote demonstrates the power of language in creating story and creating meaning. Throughout the novel, Rushdie uses imaginative language to create and veil the novel's magical world. By creating fantastical language, Rushdie is also creating something that went without a name before. This, he argues, is the power of story. It is able to bring meaning where, before, there was none.

*"'But but but what is the point of giving persons Freedom of Speech,' declaimed
Butt the Hoopoe, 'if you then say they must not utilize same? And is not the Power of
Speech the greatest Power of all? Then surely it must be exercised to the full?"*

Haroun and the Sea of Stories, 119

The tension between freedom of speech and censorship is at the heart of the war
between the Land of Gup and the Land of Chup. This tension comes out of
Rushdie's own biography. As a novelist, a fatwa was issued against him for his
characterization of Muslims in one of his novels. This attempt at silencing a free,
artistic voice provides background for the meaning of *Haroun and the Sea of
Stories*. Rushdie does want to explore the limits of freedom of speech, however. In
this passage, the army of Gup borders on mutinous behavior by questioning
authority. In the end, the freedom that Gup has proves to be the key to their victory
over the Chupwala army.

*"The Chupwalas...turned out to be a disunited rabble. Just as Mudra the Shadow
Warrior had predicted, many of them actually had to fight their own, treacherous
shadows! And as for the rest, well, their vows of silence and their habits of secrecy
had made them suspicious and distrustful of one another...The upshot was that the
Chupwalas did not stand shoulder to shoulder, but betrayed one another, stabbed on
another in the back, mutinied, hid deserted...."*

Haroun and the Sea of Stories, 185

This description of the end of the Chupwala army illustrates Rushdie's point that a
political society of censorship and authoritarian control can never stand when truly
challenged. Because the people of Chup had been silenced by Khattam-Shud and
because they had abandoned the narrative of their past and present, they proved to
be no match for the free and talkative Guppees. The Chupwalas are meant to
symbolize the destructive authoritarian regimes of the Middle East and Asia.
Rushdie criticizes this rule as being nothing more than a shadow that will turn
against its owner during difficult times.

*"'Really, this is beginning to look like a war between buffoons,' thought Rashid the
storyteller as he put on his false red nose."*

Haroun and the Sea of Stories, 179

This line represents Rushdie's view of war as an errand of foolishness. Though the
Guppee army goes to fight for what seems to be noble causes, the result of war is
ultimately a sad and destructive path. By wearing clown noses, Rushdie compares
the armaments of battle to the disguise of the fool. In a previous passage, Rashid

notes that war creates crudeness out of what seemed refined. It is important to note that these thoughts all come from Rashid the storyteller. Rashid, in this instance, represents the need for story to communicate the real meaning of war.

"Outside, in the living room, his mother had begun to sing."
Haroun and the Sea of Stories, 211

Song plays an integral role in the novel. This alludes to the fact that, in ancient times, story was communicated orally through song. Orality, therefore, is important for the communication of ideas and personality. In this final line of the novel, Haroun's mother closes the story with a song. This represents the fact that there is never truly an ending to any story. The story of life, even the life of the story itself, continues in the collective imaginations of those that hear it and embody its meaning.

"'Happy endings must come at the end of something,' the Walrus pointed out. 'If they happen in the middle of a story, or an adventure, or the like, all they do is cheer things up for a while.'"
Haroun and the Sea of Stories, 202

This quote continues to expand on the idea of a story's end by questioning the value of the happy ending. It could be argued that *Haroun and the Sea of Stories* does not end with a traditional happy ending, though the conflict of the novel has been made right in the final pages. There is still a measure of melancholy in Haroun as he doubts the realness of his own happy ending. Rushdie is attempting to explain that no story ever truly has a happy ending, especially when it is a continuing story such as life. The resolution of conflict is only a temporary happiness in the journey of the story.

"'Thanks to the genius of the Eggheads at P2C2E House,' Butt began, taking pity on Haroun, 'the rotation of Kahani has been brought under control. As a result the Land of Gup is bathed in Endless Sunshines, while over in Chup it's always the middle of the night."
Haroun and the Sea of Stories, 80

It is clear by the end of the novel that Rushdie is firmly on the side of the open society, free speech, and cultural advancement represented by the Land of Gup. However, he does not endorse this without criticism. This quote illustrates how it is the very technology, advancement, and enlightenment of the Guppee society that created the darkness of the Land of Chup, which they now oppose. This process represents the way in which advanced Western societies, through their endorsement of cultures of control in other parts of the world, have brought about many of the ills that they now must fight. The issue of terrorism is briefly alluded to in the novel and is an example of an evil that Western nations directly or indirectly caused and that they now fight.

"This is an affair of the heart."

Haroun and the Sea of Stories, 43

The overarching narrative of the novel is a love story. It is a story between the love between a father and a son and between a husband and a wife. Other stories appear in the narrative -- princess rescue stories, friendship stories, and heroic adventures -- but over all them is the motivation of a son to care for his father and reunite his family. The end of the novel and the return of Haroun's mother confirm this. The happy ending, in as far as there is one, is the recovery of love in a broken situation. The greatest motivation of any narrative or story, Rushdie suggests, is love.

Summary and Analysis of Chapters 1-2

Summary

Chapter 1 - The Shah of Blah

The novel opens in the "saddest of cities" in the country of Alifbay. The city stands "by a mournful sea full of glumfish" and all the people are full of sadness and melancholy. Haroun Khalifa lives in the middle of this city with his father and mother. His father, Rashid, is a famous storyteller. "To his admirers he was Rashid the Ocean of Notions, as stuffed with cheery stories as the sea was full of glumfish; but to his jealous rivals he was the Shah of Blah." Haroun and his family live a happy life in the city, until one day, when something goes wrong.

Rashid travels a lot because his cheery stories are in demand. His stories are fantastical, full of strange characters and dramatic situations. Haroun often wonders where his father gets all these stories since "stories can't simply come out of thin air." His father will only say that all his stories come from the great Story Sea. Haroun continues to ask these questions of his father all the time until one day, Haroun asks "one question too many, and then all hell broke loose."

Haroun is an only child, a strange circumstance in a city where there are mostly big families. Even stranger are the Senguptas, the Khalifa's upstairs neighbors, who have no children at all. Mrs. Sengupta often treats Haroun as if he were her own son. Sometimes Haroun likes this and sometimes he does not. Mr. Sengupta dislikes Haroun's father and sometimes he launches into criticisms of Rashid, telling Haroun's mother that Rashid has "his head stuck in the air and his feet off the ground. What are all these stories? Life is not a storybook or a joke shop...What's the use of stories that aren't even true?"

One day, Haroun returns from school in a downpour and sees Mrs. Sengupta standing upstairs crying. Inside his house, he finds his father crying as well and he learns that his mother has run off with Mr. Sengupta. In a fit of anger, Rashid breaks every clock in the house, stopping them at 11 o'clock sharp. The letter that Haroun's mother leaves accuses Rashid of having no room for facts in his mind. Haroun becomes angry with his father and yells at him, "What's the point of it? *What's the use of stories that aren't even true?*" Haroun realizes immediately that he should not have said that, and he blames himself when, soon afterwards, Rashid stands up in front of an audience to tell a story and no words come out.

Haroun finds it hard to concentrate on anything for longer than eleven seconds and Mrs. Sengupta thinks that the eleven seconds is significant since that is the time Haroun's mother left. She diagnosis his problem as located in his "pussy-collar-jee." They realize she means, *psychology*, and so Rashid decides to take his son with him on a story-telling job for some politicos. Rashid is often hired by politicians to tell flattering stories about them so that they will win their elections. They go to the Town of G, which "is not so special," to tell the stories. When Rashid goes out to perform, he again finds no words to tell his story. He can only say, "Ark, ark, ark." The politicos are angry and tell him that he must go to the Valley of K and tell stories there or else they will cut out his tongue. Haroun knows he must do something because this is all his fault.

Chapter 2 - The Mail Coach

At the bus station, Haroun and Rashid jostle in a crowd for a chance to buy a ticket to the Valley of K. There are signs all over the station that say things like "If you try to rush or zoom / you are sure to meet your doom," or "All the dangerous overtakers / end up safe at undertaker's." The bus depot is a crowded place because there are too many passengers and not enough buses.

Haroun runs into a man who he thinks looks something like a parrot. The man tells him his name is Butt, "driver of the Number One Super Express Mail Coach to the Valley of K." Haroun as an idea and asks Butt if he will take him and his father to see the beauty of the road from the Town of G to the Valley of K, a road that climbs "like a serpent through the Pass of H towards the Tunnel of I." Mr. Butt protests that it is late, but decides that he will fulfill the young man's request.

The mail coach drives at great speed down the road to the Valley of K. They pass bins of mail that they should pick up. Butt tells them, "Need's a slippery snake, that's what it is...it's been said of me that Butt Needs Speed, but but but it may be that my heart truly needs a Different Sort of Thrill. O, Need's a funny fish: it makes people untruthful." Many of the passengers beg Butt to slow down, but Butt only speeds up. Haroun worries that he has doomed all the passengers with his request to see the Valley of K.

As they climb up into the mountains, Haroun has the feeling that he is going to be "wiped out, like a word on a blackboard, one swoosh of the duster and I'll be gone for good." The bus goes through a bank of clouds, Butt hits the brakes very hard, and Haroun thinks that this is it...and suddenly they are in the tunnel and out with a view of the Valley of K in front of them.

It is a beautiful valley. Their journey reminds Rashid of *khattam-shud*, "the Arch-Enemy of all Stories, even of Language itself. He is the Prince of Silence and the Foe of Speech." Haroun thinks that the view is helping his father since his crazy stories are returning. The bus slowly makes its way down the mountain and Haroun sees a sign "daubed with crude, irregular letters" that reads "Welcome to Kosh-Mar." Rashid admits that "Kosh-Mar" is the word for "nightmare" in the old tongue.

K is a remote place and so news of Rashid's storytelling problems have not yet reached the politicos there. Mr. Buttoo, one of the political bosses of the valley, meets Rashid and Haroun. He is a very slick man. Haroun does not trust him. They are all protected by exactly one hundred and one heavily armed soldiers. Haroun thinks about telling his father that they should leave, but he does not get the chance. A luxurious swan boat picks them up on the shores of Dull Lake to take them across. Mr. Buttoo can tell Rashid looks sad and he tells him, "She may have you *but there are plenty more fish in the sea.*" Rashid only answers, "Ah, but you must go a long, long way to find an Angel Fish." A hot wind begins to blow and a thick mist comes in so that they can barely see anything.

Analysis

Haroun and the Sea of Stories is a novel that functions on two levels. On the base level, it is an adventure novel written for young adults. In interviews, Rushdie explained that he wrote the novel with his own children in mind. He developed many of the stories by telling them extemporaneously to his children during bath time. The novel's audience, therefore, is children. On a second level, the book is a commentary on literature and literary culture written for adults. It has meanings and inside jokes that most children will not understand. It contains certain themes that function on the level of adult consciousness.

Haroun Khalifa is the novel's eponymous hero. The opening chapter introduces Haroun and presents the novel's overarching conflict. Haroun's family breaks apart because Haroun and his mother both question Rashid Khalifa's storytelling and perspective on reality. This causes Rashid to lose his ability to tell stories. This gift is his livelihood and his reason for existing. Haroun realizes that he has crushed his father and broken his spirit. The novel's action revolves around Haroun's quest to reclaim his father's storytelling gift.

Throughout the novel, Rushdie uses a great amount of alliteration, rhyme, and made-up words to create a playfulness of language. This playfulness helps to create the fantastical world to which Haroun travels. It also helps the reader note that the setting for this story is not the same real world that the reader inhabits. It is, instead, a world that closely resembles the reader's world. In literature, this classifies the novel as a work of "magical realism." This aesthetic style blends fantastical and magical elements of a story into a realistic setting. This blending of the fantastical and the real allows the author to explore the deeper meaning of reality.

The opening setting is in the "sad city." The city is unnamed except for its emotion because the people have forgotten the name of the city. The act of naming is a theme throughout the novel. In a later chapter, Iff the Water Genie tells Haroun that to name a thing is to bring it into being. The opposite is also true -- to lose a thing or place name means that an essential identity of it is lost. This is the case for the "sad city." The city is Rushdie's commentary on the collision between the ancient and the modern. Modernity is represented by the city's industrial advance. One of the results of modernity is that it strips the essential identity from culture.

Haroun and the Sea of Stories can be classified as following the narrative of the heroic tale. In such tales, first developed in Classical Greek literature, the hero of the story goes on a quest to find his home and to restore order to the world. While on the journey, the hero faces numerous challenges that threaten to doom him and his journey. The story climaxes in an epic battle between good and evil. This overarching narrative frames the novel.

Summary and Analysis of Chapters 3-4

Summary

Chapter 3

There is unhappiness in the air of Dull Lake. It smells terrible and all think that someone has made a stink. Haroun realizes this must be Moody Land. Moody Land is a fantastical land from his father's stories. In Moody Land, the weather changes according to the mood of the people. Haroun sees that his father is so sad that it has brought the Mist of Misery. Mr. Snooty Buttoo is so full of hot air that he has brought a boiling wind.

The waters begin to rock and the oarsmen cry out that the boat is going to sink. Haroun tells everyone to think of the most pleasant thoughts they know. As soon as they do, the waters calm and the "malodorous mist" breaks. Haroun now knows "that the real world is full of magic, so magical worlds could easily be real."

Mr. Buttoo's houseboat is called *Arabian Nights Plus One*. Inside there are elaborate decorations and luxurious rooms. In the library, there are shelves of books (though most of the books are fake). In the middle of Rashid's bedroom, there is an enormous wooden peacock that is removed to reveal a large bed. Haroun's room has a large turtle that does the same thing. Haroun says the accommodations are "very pleasant," which infuriates Mr. Buttoo who wishes that Haroun call the boat "Super-Marvelloso, Incredibable, and wholly Fantastick."

Haroun and Rashid both find it difficult to sleep in their respective beds and so they decide to trade. Rashid is mostly worried that he will get up on stage the next day and have nothing to say but "ark." In the new room, Haroun dozes off and then hears some commotion in his bathroom. He wakes to see an astonishing figure; it has "an outsize onion for a head and outsize aubergines for legs." It holds a toolbox and mumbles. Haroun sneaks over to the bathroom and listens to his mutterings.

The figure is an old man wearing a purple turban and baggy silk pajamas. He is muttering about how he is being forced to uninstall something at the last minute because a subscription ran out and how he does not have time for such things. Haroun accidentally steps on a creaky board and the old man looks up, spins around several times, and disappears. As he leaves, he drops a wrench on the floor.

Haroun grabs the wrench. It is a strange tool, "it had the general outline of a wrench, but it was somehow more fluid than solid." Slowly the old man rematerializes in front of Haroun. The old man demands the wrench back, but Haroun refuses. The old man tells Haroun that he is the Water Genie, Iff from the Ocean of the Streams of Story. He is there to turn off the Story Water from the Great Story Sea because "the gentleman no longer requires the service; has discontinued narrative activities, thrown in the towel, packed it in." Haroun is shocked at the thought that his father has thrown off the Story Stream and asks how the genie knows his father is quitting. Iff tells him it the news was sent by a "P2C2E" (Process Too Complicated To Explain) involving Thought Beams.

Haroun asks how the order can be reversed and Iff tells him to take the issue up with the Grand Comptroller at P2C2E House, Gup City, Kahani. All letters must be addressed to the Walrus. Iff explains that many brilliant people, the Eggheads, are employed at Gup City but that only the Walrus is the Grand Comptroller. Iff reveals the invisible story water tap to Haroun and Haroun then makes the "most important decision of his life." He asks Mr. Iff to take him to Gup City to see the Comptroller. Iff initially refuses, but when Haroun threatens to keep his wrench, he relents and tells Haroun they must leave that night.

Chapter 4

The Water Genie tells Haroun to pick a bird, though there are no birds around. The Genie says that just by saying the bird's name, he can summon it, even if it is not a real creature. "To give a thing a name, a label, a handle; to rescue it from anonymity, to pluck it out of the Place of Namelessness, in short to identify it--well, that's a way of bringing the said thing into being." Haroun tell the Genie that this does not happen in the real world. The Genie answers, "Believe in your own eyes and you'll get into a lot of trouble, hot water, a mess."

The Genie pulls out a handful of tiny, magical bird creatures and tells Haroun to pick one. Haroun is amazed and picks the Hoopoe, the "bird that leads all other birds through many dangerous places." The Genie throws the Hoopoe out the window and into the water where it balloons to a huge size. Haroun and the Water Genie jump onto the Hoopoe's back and suddenly it accelerates through the air to a speed so fast "that the Earth below them and the sky above them both dissolved into a blur."

Looking at the Hoopoe, Haroun cannot help but think it looks much like Mr. Butt from the mail coach. Hearing Haroun's thoughts, the Hoopoe turns around and telepathically speaks to him. Haroun gives the bird the name of "Butt." Haroun sees a moon in the distance and Butt tells Haroun that this is Kahani, the Earth's second Moon. Kahani is only visible because of "Speed" which "brings light to reveal" but can also be used to conceal. Kahani travels so fast that Earth's instruments cannot detect it; the moon moves in various trajectories to make sure that Story Water is evenly distributed throughout the planet. Butt glides in for a landing on Kahani in the middle of a giant sea.

Haroun wonders why they land in the middle of an ocean, and the Water Genie tells him it is to facilitate a bureaucratic shortcut. By drinking Wishwater from the sea, Haroun's desire for his father's storytelling to return can be accomplished without having to see the Walrus. They find the water and Haroun takes a gulp. He feels a golden glow all around him and tries to wish for his father's storytelling to come back. When he does, however, he only sees an image of his mother. He hears his father crying to help him, but he cannot fully concentrate on the wish. After eleven minutes, his concentration is broken and the golden glow goes away.

Butt decides that Haroun needs a "cheering up procedure." The sea is full of a thousand different currents, the Streams of Story. These are "all the stories that had ever been told and many that were still in the process of being invented." Iff dips into the Ocean and produces a golden cup with a story inside. Haroun drinks the water and finds himself looking through the eyes of a young hero in a land full of monsters and strange things. There is a princess in a tower and Haroun watches as the hero dispenses with the monsters and begins to climb the tower. Haroun is in "Princes Rescue Story Number S/1001/ZHT/420/41(r)xi." Halfway up the tower, the hero begins to turn into a spider and when he reaches the top, the princes begins to hack away at the horrible creature until the hero falls to the ground.

Haroun wakes from the story and tells his friends of the awful ending. Iff tells Haroun that the Ocean has become polluted by the leader of the Land of Chup, "on the Dark Side of Kahani." The leader's name is Khattam-Shud.

Analysis

Rushdie borrows themes from numerous literary works. One of the most often referenced works in the novel is *One Thousand and One Arabian Nights.* This work of stories and folktales originally written during the Islamic Golden Age (mid-8th to mid-13th centuries C.E.) is considered the classic example of Eastern folktale. Throughout the novel, there are numerous references to the number one thousand and one, the first being Mr. Snooty Buttoo's boat. In addition, the names of Haroun and Rashid allude to the same work. Haroun al-Rashid is a recurring hero in the *Arabian Nights*.

There are also multiple references to Kashmir, which points towards the real setting on which Rushdie bases his fantastical land. Kashmir is a disputed piece of land on the border of India and Pakistan. Rushdie has roots in Pakistan and considers it a homeland. The Valley of K is a reference to Kashmir, as is the "Dull Lake," a variance on Dahl Lake, which is found in Kashmir. The political situation in Kashmir is also fictionalized. Mr. Snooty Buttoo represents the authoritarian government that currently rules Pakistan. This government, Rushdie suggests, manipulates the people in order to stay in power. Rushdie explores this theme of cultural manipulation further in the novel.

The appearance of Iff the Water Genie is another allusion to *One Thousand and One Arabian Night.* One of the most famous tales in that work is "Aladdin's Wonderful Lamp," in which a young boy is given a ring with a genie inside that does the bidding of those that command it. In the same way, Iff is forced to do the bidding of Haroun because Haroun holds his magic wrench. Another character introduced her is Butt the Hoopoe, a mechanical bird capable of telepathy and flying at impossible speeds. Because the Hoopoe uses the same alliteration of speech ("but but but") and shares similar physical characteristics to Butt the mail coach driver, Haroun gives the Hoopoe the same name.

The setting of the novel shifts to Kahani, the earth's second moon and source of the Sea of Stories. Kahani is where all of earth's stories originate. They are distributed throughout the world by the forces of gravity. The moon travels at the speed of light. This speed allows light to be revealed, but it also allows things to be concealed since they move so fast that the human eye cannot see it. The theme of revealing and concealing with light recurs throughout the novel. Kahani is Hindi for "story."

Haroun's adventure in the princess rescue story is an allusion to the classic tale of "Rapunzel," in which a prince must climb a tower to rescue a princess. In the traditional story, the prince uses the princess's hair to climb the tower. "Rapunzel" is the classic narrative of rescue. This story is an example of the framing narrative in which a story is framed within the narrative of another story. This is a technique used in many classic folk tales including *One Thousand and One Arabian Nights*. In this case, Haroun becomes part of an adventure tale through the mechanism of a dream while also being a part of another adventure tale in his non-dream life.

Summary and Analysis of Chapters 5-6

Summary

Chapter 5

Haroun and Iff the Water Genie speed along the Ocean of Stories on the back of Butt the Hoopoe. Haroun tries to find out more about Khattam-Shud from Iff. Iff tells him just what his father had told him: Khattam-Shud is "the Arch-Enemy of all Stories...the Prince of Silence and the Foe of Speech." He adds that most of what is known about Khattam-Shud is "gossip and flim-flam, because it's been generations since any of us went across the Twilight Strip into the Perpetual Night." Because of Kahani's rotation, a process generated by Guppee Eggheads, the Land of Gup is always in Endless Sunshine. In Chup, where Khattam-Shud resides, it is always the middle of the night. The Twilight Strip and the invisible Chattergy's Wall divide the two.

They enter busy Gup City. Iff finds out that all units have been ordered back to base, but he did not get the message. A strange looking weed comes speeding along beside their boat. Butt tells Haroun that it is "A Floating Gardener," and the weed transforms itself into the likeness of a person right before Haroun's eyes. It runs across the surface of the water showing no signs of sinking. Mali, the Floating Gardener, untwists the stories in the water. Iff explains that as the stories grow longer, they also become twisted and braided. Mali tells Haroun that the pollution in the ocean is become very bad. "Certain popular romances have become just long lists of shopping expeditions. Children's stories also. For instance, there is an outbreak of talking helicopter anecdotes."

A group of Angel Fish comes to the surface. They are "as big as sharks" with "literally dozens of mouths." Butt tells Haroun that these are Plentimaw Fishes (named because "they have plenty of maws, i.e., mouths"). These fish are always in pairs with their faithful partners for life. They look very sick because of the pollution. The fish swallow the stories in the sea and then miracles occur in their innards; "a little bit of one story joins on to an idea from another...when they spew the stories out they are not old tales but new ones." Iff tells Haroun, "No story comes from nowhere; new stories are born from old--it is the new combinations that make them new." The pollution is especially bad in the Old Zone, a place known as the Source of Stories, near the Moon's South Pole.

Everyone in Gup City goes to the Lagoon, "a beautiful expanse of multicolored waters." There are gigantic buildings all around, including the P2C2E House. Iff and Haroun walk to the Pleasure Garden where there are large numbers of dressed in rectangular garments covered in writing. These are the Pages of Gup, the city's army. They are organized into Chapters and Volumes which is headed by a Title Page. The entire Library (or, army) is headed by General Kitab, who stands on a balcony on the Palace of Gup. Next to him is the Speaker of the Chatterbox and King Chattergy, a frail looking old man. Next to them are two other gentlemen. One is an agitated young man, Prince Bolo, "the fiance of King Chattergy's only child, his daughter the Princess Batcheat," and a man with a bald head and "a disappointingly insignificant mustache that looked like a piece of a dead mouse." This is the Walrus. All the people around him hear Haroun ask about the man. They all have bald heads and wear white lab coats. They are the Eggheads. They tell Haroun that the man is called the Walrus because of his "thick, luxuriant walrus mustache." Haroun thinks, "I suppose if you're as hairless as these Eggheads...even that pathetic dead mouse on the Walrus's upper lip looks like the greatest thing you've ever seen."

Prince Bolo speaks to the crowd. Princess Batcheat is missing. The people of Chup have kidnapped her. The Speaker says that messages have been sent to Chup, but now a time of war has come. The Walrus tells the crowd that the Ocean and Batcheat are in grave danger. Iff asks for his disconnector since the Walrus will have no time to see Haroun now. Haroun refuses and Iff hands him a bar of chocolate. The people of Kahani have to get any "tasty and wicked luxury" foods from earth. Haroun realizes that this is where Unidentified Flying Objects come from.

There is a commotion amongst the leaders on the balcony. A spy has been caught in the Twilight Area. The spy is brought forth before the crowd. He is wearing a blue nightgown and a hood. The hood is removed, and Haroun is shocked to see his father, Rashid Khalifa.

Chapter 6

Rashid proclaims that he is only a storyteller, a subscriber to the Story Water. Haroun pushes his way through the crowd. He wonders what punishment the people of Gup will give his father. Iff says that they have never actually caught a spy before; they will probably make him write, "I must not spy," one thousand and one times, though maybe that is too severe. Haroun comes before his father and tells everyone, "The only thing wrong with him is that he's lost the Gift of the Gab."

A Page escorts Haroun away from the crowd. The Page's name is Blabbermouth. Haroun reads the story written on the Page's uniform. It is "Bolo and the Golden Fleece," a story that Haroun thinks he remembers being about someone else. Other Pages in the palace also have familiar, yet altered, stories written on them: "'Bolo and the Wonderful Lamp'...'Bolo and the Forty Thieves'...'Bolo the Sailor', 'Bolo and Juliet', 'Bolo in Wonderland.'" They go to the Throne Room where Prince Bolo, General Kitab, the Speaker, and the Walrus are gathered around Rashid.

Rashid begins his story. He had been looking for a special concoction of food that cures his insomnia. The food carries the eater to Rapture where "a person may choose to wake up in the place to which the dream takes him; to wake up, that is to say, *inside the dream.*" He goes to Gup, but because of a miscalculation, he ends up in the Twilight Strip where he almost freezes to death. Bad things are happening in the Twilight Strip. There is an encampment of the Chupwala Army, "black tents, wrapped in such a fanatical silence!" The Land of Chup has fallen under the power of the "Mystery of Bezaban,...a Cult of Dumbness or Muteness." In this cult, Khattam-Shud declares hatred against stories. Now he "opposes Speech for any reason at all." There are members of the Mystery that sew their lips together and they die of hunger and thirst as sacrifices to Bezaban. Rashid explains that Bezaban is a giant idol made of ice. It is in Khattam-Shud's palace. It is a frightful idol.

There are many soliders in the Twilight Strip now. They come into Gup through holes in Chattergy's Wall. While in the Twilight Strip, Rashid saw a young woman with the worst singing voice he had ever heard, come in a swan boat. Iff explains that the young people of Gup often go to the Twilight Strip because, "It is a daredevil thing to do...Dark has its fascinations: mystery, strangeness, romance." The Princess wanted to touch Chattergy's Wall. As she and her handmaidens go to touch it, the Chupwala Army seizes her. Rashid relays the message that the Army is planning to sacrifice her to Bezaban during the Great Feast to the god." Bolo declares war on Chup and Rashid offers to show them the Chupwala tents.

Haroun becomes very tired and Blabbermouth leads him out of the Throne Room and to his room to rest. They become lost in the palace because Blabbermouth talks incessantly about her dislike of Princess Batcheat and of how she changed all the stories on their uniforms so that the hero was always Bolo, her fiancé. Haroun, upset that they are lost, knocks the hat off of Blabbermouth's head. Long dark hair falls out and Haroun realizes that Blabbermouth is a girl. She is indignant at Haroun's surprise. "You think it's easy for a girl to get a job like this? Don't you know girls have to fool people every day of their lives if they want to get anywhere?" Blabbermouth hits a button in a closet, and they are suddenly transported to the roof where they gaze out on the Pleasure Garden and the Land of Gup. Haroun realizes, "he had never felt more completely alive in his life...." Blabbermouth takes out balls of golden silk from her pocket and begins to juggle. She adds more and more balls until she is juggling a dozen or more. This is like storytelling, Haroun thinks. "You keep a lot of different tales in the air, and juggle them up and down, and if you're good you don't drop any."

Haroun wakes up hours later. There is a heavy weight on his chest and someone is squeezing his neck tightly. It is Blabbermouth, who warns him not to tell anyone about her or she will squeeze harder next time he is asleep. He agrees. Blabbermouth tells him to get up and get ready because the Gup army is ready to march.

Analysis

There is a strong autobiographical theme to *Haroun and the Sea of Stories*. In 1989, Ayatollah Ruhollah Khomeini, the leader of Iran, issued a death fatwa against Salman Rushdie for his depiction of Islam in his award winning novel *The Satanic Verses*. The fatwa meant that Rushdie was forced into protective isolation. Admittedly, he went into a prolonged period of writer's block because of the situation. *Haroun and the Sea of Stories* was Rushdie's first novel following the fatwa.

Rushdie uses the power of Khattam-Shud as the symbol for this difficult period of his life. Khattam-Shud is the antagonist of the novel, but it is also a concept larger than a single character. Khattam-Shud is the antithesis of story; it is complete silence. This is not simply a matter of condemning or criticizing a work of art. It is, instead, an act of dictatorial control through a total silencing of an author and artist. This theme of silence is explored in many different angles through the novel. Rushdie even includes himself in the novel. "Rashid" is a very close anagram to "Rushdie," a sly nod that Rushdie is himself the storyteller that has had his heart broken and his gift taken from him.

This tension between silence and story is symbolized between the competing lands of Gup and Chup. Gup is Hindi for "gossip" or "nonsense." This represents the fact that the Guppees exist in one extreme spectrum of the propensity for speech. They talk so much that their talk begins to lose its efficacy and meaning. On the other extreme of the spectrum is Chup, which is Hindi for "quiet." In Chup, silence has been ordered. Some take it to such an extreme that they sew their lips together and sacrifice themselves by starving and thirsting to death.

Rushdie often alludes to Lewis Carroll's *Alice's Adventures in Wonderland*. Rushdie's Haroun follows a journey very similar to that of Alice; he is transported to a dreamlike land with the aid of a magical creature where he must fight an evil ruler in order to restore the land to its right state and then return home. One of the most humorous allusions is the description of the Guppee army, or "Library." Just as in *Alice* the Queen's army is made of cards, here the Guppee army represents the propensity for story and speech. The members of the army are dressed as pages with stories written on them. The stories have been changed, however. This symbolizes the fact that even benevolent rulers contain the desire to usurp a legend's meaning for their own gain.

Although Gup and Chup both fall on extreme ends of a spectrum of speech, Rushdie is careful not to let these lands fall at the extreme ends of a spectrum of good and evil. Factors such as the manipulation of stories, the secrecy of the Walrus and the Eggheads, and the questionable reasoning for casting darkness over Chup all suggest that Gup is not the embodiment of goodness. In fact, as will be seen in a forthcoming chapter, any land that participates in war cannot be entirely benevolent and good. Likewise, Chup is initially seen to be evil and destructive. Haroun, however, will find a sense of beauty in the darkness of the land.

Summary and Analysis of Chapters 7-8

Summary

Chapter 7

Haroun realizes that by volunteering to help save Batcheat, he is becoming caught in another princess rescue story. Blabbermouth tells him that she removed the Disconnecting Tool from under his pillow while he was asleep. Haroun thinks that everything is ruined, but Blabbermouth tells him that his father can work out his own problems with the Walrus. Haroun tells her that she does not understand: "I wanted to do it for him."

All of the Pages in the army are jostling to find out their order. Haroun thinks this should be easy, since they are numbered, but Blabbermouth tells him that he should not "judge a book by its cover," as there are chapters and volumes that must be taken into account. Haroun and Blabbermouth make it to the Garden, and Haroun sees his father, disheveled and wearing his nightshirt, in a pavilion standing with Iff the Water Genie. The Army gives a cry of, "For Batcheat and the Ocean," and they begin to march. Rashid, Iff, and Haroun climb aboard Butt the Hoopoe and they go.

Rashid laments that they will freeze in their nightshirts, but Iff gives them Laminations, transparent garments that cling to them so tightly that they do not even feel that they are wearing them. Haroun is amazed at how quickly his life has changed. "It's a case of out of the frying pan into the fire." Butt the Hoopoe answers that it is more a case of "out of the fridge into the freezer." Rashid is amazed that the machine spoke without moving its beak.

There is a great noise in the army and Haroun realizes it is all the Pages arguing about the cause for the war. Some think it is to save Batcheat; others think it is to save the Ocean. Haroun thinks that this sounds like mutinous talk, but mutiny is a concept no one understands. Haroun explains that it is an adjective, another concept that the Guppees do not understand. General Kitab flies around the army listening to the arguments and even provoking the disputes. Haroun thinks that earth soldiers would be court marshaled for such talk, but Butt the Hoopoe wonders what the use of Freedom of Speech is if it cannot be used. The army marches on, discussing the General's secret plans (which he divulged to everyone, of course). Only Prince Bolo remains aloof and Haroun wonders why. Mali, the Floating Gardener, tells him it is because of love, a "wonderful and dashing matter. But which can also be a very foolish thing."

As the army enters the Twilight Strip, Haroun despairs that it is all a suicidal mission. Butt tells him that he is suffering a "Heart-Shadow," which happens to everyone the first time they see the Darkness beyond. As they enter Chup, the poison in the water becomes worse and the currents are no longer warm. The Guppees land on the shores, but there are no attacks against them. After establishing a beachhead, Kitab and Bolo fetch Rashid to lead them towards the Princess.

They move into a small clearing where they see a man who looks "almost like a shadow" with a sword. As they near, they realize that it is a man fighting his own shadow. The shadow's movements do not match the man's, and they leap and dodge each other. The warrior is frightening, with a green painted face, thick leather battle armor, and black eyes with grey irises. Haroun thinks that this is a battle of opposites, "Gup is bright and Chup is dark. Gup is warm and Chup is freezing cold. Gup is all chattering and noise, whereas Chup is silent as a shadow...a war between Love and Death." However, Haroun also sees a beauty in the graceful battle movements of the Chup soldier, a sign that "silence has its own grace and beauty (just as speech could be graceless and ugly)." The warrior realizes that someone is watching him and he sends his shadow to the bushes. The shadow's hands begin moving furiously and then it begins to speak.

Chapter 8

The Shadow Warrior begins to croak out unintelligible words. Bolo demands to know what the man is saying and Blabbermouth quietly calls him a poser, an opinion that makes Haroun question why she chooses to follow such a man. Rashid explains that it is not uncommon for those who have not used their voices in a long time to lose control of it. The Warrior repeats the phrase "Murder, Spock Obi New Year," and Rashid realizes he is telling them that his name is Mudra and that he speaks in the ancient Gesture Language of Abhinaya, which Rashid understands. He begins to interpret the Warrior's gestures.

They learn that the Warrior is second in command to Khattam-Shud but that he has become disgusted with the war and violence. Most Chupwalas do not follow Khattam-Shud or worship Bezaban, but instead live in fear. If Khattam-Shud is defeated, Chupwalas would be in favor of peace. Mudra explains that in Chup, a person's Shadow is their equal. It can change shapes and forms and sometimes is even dominant over its "Substance or Self or Person." Peace means that each Chupwala is at peace with their Shadows. Khttam-Shud's black magic has caused his Shadow to separate from him, and it goes wherever it wishes. Defeating Khattam-Shud means also defeating his shadow.

Kitab asks for Mudra's help and Mudra agrees. He tells them that they must make a decision -- which Khattam-Shud do they fight first. One is in the Old Zone poisoning the Ocean while the other holds Batcheat captive. Prince Bolo tells them that life is most important so they must save Batcheat. General Katib reluctantly agrees but tells them that someone should go and spy on Khattam-Shud in the Old Zone. Haroun bravely stands up and volunteers. He tells them all that he had grown up hearing the stories but that he never believed they were true. Now that he has seen all of Kahani, he does not "like the idea that all the good stories in the world will go wrong for ever and ever, or just die." Haroun thinks that maybe it is not too late to save the ocean.

Bolo slaps Haroun on the back and tells everyone that he is the man for the job because he is "a slave to Love."

Haroun, Mali the Gardner, Butt the Hoopoe, Iff the Water Genie, and the Pentimaw Fishes trek towards the Old Zone. The water becomes more and more poisonous the further they go and soon the Pentimaw Fish tell them they cannot go on. Haroun tells them to stay back and keep watch. They reach a kind of forest standing on the Ocean. Mali tells them that it is neglected water. He jumps into the overgrown brush and begins cutting a path. Strange creatures fly out of the weed-jungle. When the channel is clear, they enter. Suddenly a great net flies out and covers them. It is a Web of Night, futile to resist. Black eyes peer at them through the brush and Haroun despairs that he is a very poor hero.

Analysis

Several examples of Rushdie's play with language are on display in these chapters. The first occurs in Chapter 7 when Blabbermouth tells Haroun not to "judge a book by its cover" as he observes the army. This is the use of an aphorism, a saying that embodies a general truth. In this case, the saying has a double meaning since the army is constructed in pages, chapters, and volumes just like a book. Another example is Haroun's use of the phrase, "out of the frying pan and into the fryer." This is an example of an idiom, a phrase whose meaning is not predictable from its general meaning. In this case, Haroun is saying that he has gone from one bad situation into something even worse.

One of the most striking elements of play in language is in Rushdie's use of names. Almost all of the names in *Haroun and the Sea of Stories* either allude to other stories or parts of culture, or have been derived from other words in the Hindustani language. For example, Batcheat is derived from 'baat-cheet', meaning 'chit-chat.' Bolo is derived from the verb 'Bolna,' meaning 'to speak.' Gup means 'gossip," and Mudra is the name of any gesture in the Abhinaya language, which is in fact a real Language of Gesture in Indian classical dance. The names in the novel all correspond with the essence of the culture from which the character comes. For example, all of the names of the people of Gup correspond to wordiness, gossip, or speech. The names of the people from Chup (which means 'quiet') correspond to silence or the lack of speech.

The gossip, conversation, and arguments of the Guppee army on the way to Chup is an example of one of the novel's major themes: the tension between free speech and complete silence. Though Rushdie is decisively in favor of freedom of speech and expression, Haroun's worry that the arguments of the Guppee army might cause insurrection are notable. Rushdie means for the reader to question exactly how much free speech is too much, and whether too much free speech can become counterproductive or even useless noise.

The meaning of the Old Zone and the Twilight Strip are both important concepts in the novel. The Old Zone, which is said to be the source of all stories, symbolizes the oldest source of all stories -- religious writings. It is notable that this Old Zone lies in the Twilight Strip, directly in between Chup and Gup. This Old Zone becomes the easiest place for corruption by Khattam-Shud. Again, there are biographical elements in this symbolism. Rushdie is here accusing Islamic political dictators and religious fundamentalists of poisoning the ancient religious stories. This process is what caused a death warrant to be issued for him.

The novel also deals with elements of faith and doubt. Haroun is representative of the doubting public. This loss of faith in the reality of story, Rushdie suggests, is the trajectory of society. It is not until Haroun sees Kahani with his own eyes that he believes in the stories and is motivated to action. Previously, Rashid had always acted as a conduit for the reality of the stories, but this is no longer the case.

Summary and Analysis of Chapters 9-10

Summary

Chapter 9

The Chupwalas pull Haroun, Iff, and Butt the Hoopoe forward in their nets. Butt predicts nothing but doom for them up ahead and Haroun tries to keep an optimistic outlook. There is thick acid-like poison in the Ocean now. "It's our own fault," Iff says. "We are the Guardians of the Ocean, and we didn't guard it...The oldest stories ever made...We let them rot, we abandoned them...We lost touch with our beginnings." Haroun wishes Mali were there and he is afraid that the poison has eaten the Gardner.

They reach a clearing, and Haroun sees a wall of night in front of them. He thinks that this must be the Perpetual Darkness, but it turns out that it is the hull of a colossal ship. Haroun tries to open his mouth and describe it, but the only thing that comes out is, "ark, ark." As they are led onto the ship, Butt the Hoopoe is left behind and several of the Chupwala guards unscrew his head and take out a black circuit box, the bird's brain. Iff slips Haroun a small tube. It is a Bite-a-Lite, a small device that will emit two minutes of bright light.

On the deck of the ship are rows of massive cauldrons, all containing the poison. Everything on the deck looks like shadows. It is all impermanent, as if "there was something not quite fixed or certain about it all." The whole scene looks "normal and dull" to Haroun. They are pushed to a set of double doors and when they open, a "skinny, scrawny, measly, weaselly, snivelling clerical type" comes forward. It is the Cultmaster of Bezaban, Khattam-Shud. Haroun is surprised that the man is so disappointing looking. It is an anti-climax. Haroun cannot help but think that the edges of the Cultmaster appear blurry. He realizes that this is Khattam-Shud's shadow sent from the Citadel of Chup.

Khattam-Shud tosses Butt the Hoopoe's circuit box in the air. He tells them that he will take it apart and then explain those Processes 2 Complicated 2 Explain. Haroun thinks that he recognizes Khattam-Shud and then realizes that he looks just like Mr. Sengupta, the man who stole his mother. Haroun is angry, but Iff holds him back. Khattam-Shud then changes shapes into a giant hundred foot tall monster with a hundred heads and arms. He shrinks back to normal, done showing off. He tells them, "Stories go in for such displays, but they are unnecessary and inefficient, too." Khattam-Shud takes them into the ship to see what they came to see.

Chapter 10

The ship's hull is a great cavernous space filled with darkbulbs that emit nothing but darkness. It is filled with machines "Far Too Complicated To Describe." The

Cultmaster tells them that the point of the machines is to ruin the stories of the Sea. "Each story must be ruined in a different way. To ruin a happy story, you must make it sad. To ruin an action drama, you must make it move too slowly. To ruin a mystery you must make the criminal's identity obvious even to the most stupid audience. To ruin a love story you must turn it into a tale of hate. To ruin a tragedy you must make it capable of inducing helpless laughter." Soon, the Cultmaster tells them, the Ocean will die. Haroun asks him why he hates stories since they are so fun. The Cultmaster answers, "The world...is not for Fun...the world is for Controlling."

The Cultmaster then shows them where they build the Plug, a great mechanism that will bottle up the wellspring of stories at the bottom of the Sea. A generator in the middle of the hull produces the electricity needed for all of the ship's operations. Suddenly, a web of "bizarre rooty tendrils" enters the ship through one of the portholes. A purple flower appears and Haroun rejoices that Mali has avoided capture and made his way to the ship. Mali quickly moves to the generator and spreads his roots into every crevice and nook of the machine. It grinds to a halt.

Haroun, knowing it is his turn to act, pulls the Bite-a-Lite from under his tongue and bites it. Bright light flows forth, blinding the Chupwala guards. Haroun moves to a closet and begins putting on a protective wet suit so that he can dive into the ocean. He grabs Butt the Hoopoe's brain box from Khattam-Shud. Just as the light begins to fade, Haroun pulls on his suit and dives into the Sea.

As he falls through the Sea, he sees the Plug being constructed. Then, as he sinks lower, he sees the Source of Stores, a giant hole in the seabed. It looks like a fountain of shining light. Haroun realizes that "if he could prevent the Source from being Plugged, everything would eventually be all right again." Haroun feels desperate that he can do nothing to stop everything. His hand then brushes past a bulge in his pocket and he remembers what is there. He knows there is something he can do after all.

Haroun surfaces next to Butt the Hoopoe and he begins to try to put its brain box back inside. He crosses the wires too many times, however, and Butt the Hoopoe blows a fuse before working properly. Haroun reaches into his pocket and pulls out the vial of Wishwater that Iff had given him when he first arrived in Kahani. He drinks it and begins to wish that Kahani would once again spin on its axis in a normal way. Minutes pass and, all of a sudden, the moon begins to spin quickly, and a great wash of sunlight pours over the land. All of the Chupwala guards begin to fade away. They had only been the detached shadows of the real guards, and in the sunlight, they can no longer remain solid.

Haroun goes back to the ship, which is itself dissolving, and finds Mali and Iff hung over a cauldron of poison. The rope breaks and they fall in, but the poison itself has been hardened by the sunlight and they are unharmed. They go back to Butt the Hoopoe, but his blown fuse will not allow him to take them back. Mali begins to push and just as he runs out of energy, Goopy and Bagha the Plentimaw Fishes

Summary and Analysis of Chapters 9-10

appear and begin to tow them towards the battle between General Kitab and the real Khattam-Shud.

Analysis

The use of shadows in the novel represents a complex duality. The shadows of Khattam-Shud and his Chupwala henchmen have all become evil and thrive only in the dark. Mudra's shadow, however, remains a part of him and takes part in his quest for goodness. Shadows represent the combination of light and darkness. A shadow cannot exist without light creating it, yet it is also a measure of darkness where light otherwise exists.

The fact that the shadows have detached themselves from their owners is significant. The shadow, the combination of darkness and light, correctly exists only when it is in connection to the person or thing that casts it. This example of magical realism, when a shadow detaches itself from its owner, means that the balance of darkness and light has come undone.

Throughout the first half of the novel, shadows are always connoted as evil, pernicious, or conspiratorial. The reader realizes, however, that all of these viewpoints are seen from the Guppee point of view. The Guppees, a people that live in perpetual light, are unfamiliar with the concept of shadow and live in fear of its darkness. They do not realize there are elements of light within it. Haroun first gets a glimpse of the Chupwala viewpoint of shadow as he watches Mudra's shadow warrior dance. He notes that the dance of the warrior and the shadow is beautiful and graceful.

These chapters focus on the dark side of the shadow. Haroun confuses Perpetual Darkness with the hull of Khattam-Shud's ship. This suggests that, in fact, there is little difference between Perpetual Darkness (meaning, a spiritual and physical state of darkness, probably death) and the work of Khattam-Shud. That Haroun is unable to speak or describe this darkness is representative of the fact that death and other states of Perpetual Darkness are, in the end, unable to be described. They exist beyond the abilities of consciousness.

The Cultmaster's ambitions are revealed in these chapters. Haroun questions why he would want to take the fun out of the stories. He replies by telling Haroun that the world is not for fun, the world is made to control. This is an indictment on the political, social, and religious powers of the Mid-East that seek to control societies by strictly regulating actions and beliefs. This is also a statement of the power of story. Ultimate control, Rushdie suggests, does not come from military might or authoritarian tactics. Ultimate control is the result of the control of narrative. By controlling narrative, a person's imagination is able to be co-opted. Their abilities for independence and freedom are removed.

Summary and Analysis of Chapters 11-12

Summary

Chapter 11

The narrator of the story quickly tells of all the events that happen during the war. Because the climate in Chup is so cold, all of the soldiers are issued nosewarmers; black for the Chupwala army and red for The Pages of Gup. Rashid thinks, "This is beginning to look like a war between buffoons." The Guppees wear helmets with bright haloes of light so that they can see and blind their enemies. It is a "state-of-the-art" war in which "neither army will even be able to see properly during the fight."

A band of ambassadors arrives from Chup carrying a white flag of truce. Prince Bolo insults the party, but General Kitab demands respect. The ambassador tells them that the Cultmaster will not negotiate or give up Batcheat. He adds that she has been driving the entire land crazy with her singing. The ambassador tells them that he has been ordered to entertain them with his juggling. He takes out a number of objects and begins to juggle them. Everyone becomes so enthralled with the show that only Blabbermouth sees when he takes out a lit bomb and begins to juggle it. She quickly springs to action and takes the objects and juggles them herself, throwing the bomb off a cliff where it explodes. Blabbermouth's headgear falls off and her long hair falls out. "What a creep," she says, "He was ready to commit suicide, to get blown up right along with us."

Bolo becomes angry that Blabbermouth has been hiding her gender. He tells her that she is fired and she retorts that she quits. Hearing the fuss, Mudra steps in and tells Bolo that if he will not have such a brave soldier, then she can join his army.

At last, the battle commences. Rashid is afraid that The Pages of Gup will be torn up or burned by the Chupwalas, but the opposite proves to be true. Because the Pages had talked through everything so extensively, even to the point of anarchy, their openness created bonds of unity. On the other side, the Chupwalas silence and lack of planning created distrust and confusion. The Guppees overwhelm the opposing army.

After the battle, Rashid and Blabbermouth's thoughts turn to Haroun, and they worry for him. Prince Bolo begins calling for his princess and finds her singing an old blues song that sounds familiar to him. Bolo thinks the song is beautiful while the Chupwalas yell for her to be quiet. At that moment, the moon of Kahani begins to spin. The ground shakes and the houses and fortresses of Chup begin to fall. The great statue of Bezaban falls. The small, measly, scrawny Khattam-Shud runs out from his hiding place and the head of the statue falls on him, crushing him to bits.

Peace is declared. Mudra becomes the leader of Chup and invites Blabbermouth to stay and become an official interpreter and ambassador between the two lands. Haroun arrives with his friends and everyone is reunited. Iff is promoted to Chief Water Genie and personally turns on Rashid's story water supply. Mali is named Head Floating Gardner and the Plentimaw Fishes are given charge of cleaning up the Sea. Batcheat and Bolo are married in a large ceremony, but when she offers to sing for the crowd, everyone strenuously objects. As Haroun begins to leave, an Egghead approaches him and tells him he must see the Walrus to account for breaking all of the Complicated machinery when he wished for the moon to spin.

Chapter 12

Haroun thinks that he needs a witness so he goes to each of his friends. Each tells him that the Walrus is too important and they will not cross him. Haroun has to face the Walrus alone. He ventures into the P2C2E House. There is a crowd of Eggheads wandering everywhere and the hallways twist, turn, and are complicated. Finally, he finds the Walrus's office and goes in.

Standing in the office is the Walrus and all his friends, including Blabbermouth. They are all laughing. The Walrus tells him that they were pulling his leg, "just our little yoke," and he laughs at his own pun. The Walrus tells him that, because of his service to the nation of Gup, they will grant him whatever favor he desires. Haroun becomes unhappy and only Blabbermouth understands his mood. Haroun tells them that it is no use asking for anything "because what I really want is something nobody here can give me."

The Walrus tells him that at the end of a great adventure everyone wants the same thing: a happy ending. Haroun tells him that his happy ending can't be found in an ocean. The Walrus tells him that happy endings are rare in both stories and in life. They are the exception rather than the rule. The Eggheads, however, can synthesize a happy ending. Haroun agrees and then wishes that his sad city will have a happy ending.

It is time to go home and so Haroun and Rashid climb into Butt the Hoopoe who can transport them through time as well as space. He takes them back to the *Arabian Nights Plus One* and they both fall asleep in their beds. When they awaken, they find Snooty Buttoo calling for them to come to the rally. Haroun begs his father to remember a crazy dream from the night before, but his father ignores him. As Haroun dresses, he finds a small envelope with a note signed by all his friends. The note invites him to come to Kahani whenever he wants. Inside is a small bird, Butt the Hoopoe.

Buttoo takes them to the rally where the people look angry at having to vote for Mr. Buttoo. Rashid stands up on the stage in front of the angry crowd. Haroun is worried that his father will again fall to pieces. Instead, Rashid speaks to the crowd and tells them that today he will tell them of *Haround and the Sea of Stories*.

Rashid relates the entire story of Haroun's journey to Kahani, including the parts that he did not personally witness. As he talks about Chup and the people's unrest there, the crowd begins to turn on Mr. Buttoo. By the time the story is over, Buttoo realizes his time is up in the Valley of K and he retreats, never to be seen again. Rashid and Haroun head back to their home, even though they were not paid.

As they arrive back in the sad city it is raining, but Rashid insists on walking anyway. As he walks, he becomes very happy and begins to dance. The dancing is infectious and Haroun joins in. He realizes that everyone else in the city is also dancing. The people tell him that the rain is making them happy. Haroun realizes that the Walrus put happy endings in the rain. Haroun is distressed that these are fake happy endings since nothing else in the city has changed. A policeman tells him that the city has remembered its name: "Kahani...it means 'story' you know."

As they arrive at their house, Miss Oneeta greets them and tells them of all the good news that has happened since they left. She opens the door to their apartment and Haroun finds his mother standing there. She tells them that she made a mistake by going with the measly, weasly Mr. Sengupta. Mr. Sengupta is "khattam-shud." When Haroun wakes the next morning, there are new clothes and a new clock in his room. He remembers that it is his birthday. He looks at the clock and nods, "Time is definitely on the move again around these parts." Outside, in the house, his mother begins to sing.

Analysis

The narrator of the story appears briefly in Chapter 11, one of the only times this occurs in the novel. Because the narrator reveals him or herself, the reader is made aware of the framing technique of the novel. This narrative technique mirrors that of stories in *One Thousand and One Arabian Nights* which was a major influence on Rushdie's work. Haroun's story exists within the reality of the narrator telling the story to the reader. It is thus framed within a second story.

The narrative becomes farcical when the Guppees and Chupwalas begin their war. This is somewhat of an unexpected turn in the book. The story of war had been building throughout the novel, but when the time for battle approaches, both sides make themselves look foolishness, and the battle ends with an easy victory by the Guppees. The clown noses and funny hats that each side wears represent Rushdie's opinion that any force that begins war only makes themselves look foolish. The armaments of war are not the tools of courage. It is notable that no matter how technologically advanced the Guppee society becomes, they will still not be able to see properly in their fight because of the darkness. This is a sly condemnation of war like aggression in the technologically advanced Western World.

Rushdie also makes a brief allusion to the concept of suicide bombers when Khattam-Shud's ambassador attempts to blow himself and the Guppee leadership up with a bomb. The act of suicide bombing, in which a person willfully takes their own life and those of other innocent people by detonating explosives, was and is a major terrorism issue in Middle Eastern countries such as Pakistan. The characters in the novel deal with this issue of terrorism in the same way that people of the real world deal with it: with disbelief and dismayed wonder that anyone would be so corrupted to undertake such an act.

In many places, the novel alludes to elements of popular culture in the "real" world. The Walrus and the Eggheads allude to the Beatle's song, "I Am the Walrus." Rushdie even comes close to quoting a line from the song when he gives the full name "I.M.D. Walrus." Like the novel itself, the song is an example of musical absurdism. The names of the Plentimaw Fish, Goopy and Bagha, are also the names of the heroes in a movie by Middle Eastern director Satyajit Ray. These examples demonstrate Rushdie's combination of absurd and surrealistic popular culture into his art.

It is important to note that *Haroun and the Sea of Stories* ends with something of a doubtful happy ending. It is a happy ending in that the sad city remembers its name (Kahani) and Haroun's mother returns after she realizes that she made a mistake. Haroun also realizes that he can hold onto the value of story without the help of the Guppees of Kahani. However, there is doubt in Haroun's mind over whether such a happy ending is synthetic and manufactured by the Guppees. The reader questions whether a synthetic happy ending is really a happy ending. This fact, Rushdie suggests, means that there are actually no happy endings in real life. There is only story and the story goes on forever. The novel does not end with a "happily ever after" as most princess rescue stories end. Instead, it ends with Haroun's mother singing. This represents the continuation of song and story as a frame for all of life.

Suggested Essay Questions

1. **In the novel's opening, why is the Sad City sad?**

   The sadness of Haroun's Sad City represents the transition of the Indian sub-continent from a land of tradition into a land of commerce and industry. Rushdie judges this transition to be sad because it strips away the culture and tradition of the society. This sadness is embodied by Mr. Sengupta, who criticizes Rashid for his storytelling. Mr. Sengupta, who is characterized as an accountant and a part of the commercial and industrial rise of the land, does not understand the power or value of story.

2. **Can *Haroun and the Sea of Stories* be classified as a hero epic?**

   Rushdie's novel does follow the basic template of a hero epic. A hero epic is the story of an individual who goes through great hardships in order to achieve a goal. This is usually a return to a homeland or the recovery of a lost love. In the case of *Haroun,* both of these are true. Haroun must go through a series of adventures in which he almost fails because of danger and his own weakness. In the end, he is able to help save the stories of the Sea and reconcile his relationship with his father.

3. **Discuss some of the cultural markers that make the novel unique.**

   Rushdie incorporates a number of popular cultural markers in the novel and combines them with traditional Indian folklore to create a unique imaginary world that is infused with fantastical cultural references from both East and West. For example, Rushdie heavily borrows themes Lewis Carrol's *Through the Looking Glass.* In each novel, the meaning and efficacy of language is a slippery slope. It is able to be taken away at any time. Carrol's novel also appears in the novel's "Walrus" character and there is even a reference to the Beatles song "I am the Walrus," found on their *Magical Mystery Tour* album. These references all create a sense of journey through language and consciousness that traverses and transcends worlds.

4. **Is silence the antithesis of speech?**

   At first, the people of Gup and Haroun see the Land of Chup and its void of speech as a place antithetical to their own values as a society. The Guppees see their own values as superior. They are willing to invade Chup in order to protect those values. However, as the novel progresses, Haroun finds that there is a particular kind of beauty in silence. Silence, he finds, is a complement to free speech. Free speech, in fact, can be harmful in some instances when silence is better. The beauty of silence is best represented by Mudra, the shadow warrior.

5. **Discuss the novel's political commentary.**

   On one level, the novel can be read as a simple children's adventure tale, but Rushdie also meant for the novel to be a political allegory. The questions of silence and the efficacy of substantial things all allude to Rushdie's own political drama when a fatwa was issued against him by the Shah of Iran for his depiction of Muslims in a previous novel. Rushdie criticizes the Islamic society that the Shah had built in Iran and compares it to a land of shadows. While in the land of Perpetual Darkness, Haroun notes, "That's what shadows are like; even when they're sharp, they're never as sharp-edged as real, substantial things." Rushdie judges the fundamentalist states of the Middle East to violate the reality of human freedom and flourishing.

6. **According to the novel, how can free speech become dangerous?**

Free speech becomes a dangerous thing, according to the novel, when it becomes so free that it produces nothing but nonsense. In its quest for complete freedom of speech, Gup subjected Chup to complete darkness and silence, a reminder that freedom can sometimes be oppressive to others when not checked with responsibility. As the Guppee army sails towards Chup, Haroun is shocked that there could be such open rebellion and questioning of authority in the ranks. This is another example of how an irresponsible freedom of speech can become a basis for chaos and not freedom.

7. **Why does Mudra rebel against his homeland?**

In a way, Mudra is a symbol for Rushdie's own struggle with the culture of his homeland. After the Iranian Revolution in 1979 and the resulting rise of power of Islamic fundamentalism in countries across the Middle East, Rushdie sought to fight the oppression of speech and art through his writing. Mudra's shadow represents the culture and tradition joined to a person as though it were a separate kind of substance from the person; culture has a life of its own. Mudra's conflict is that he and his fellow Chupwala's no longer trust their shadows. Rushdie uses this symbolizes as a commentary on how the culture of the Middle East is turned against them and changed into something they can no longer trust.

8. **Is *Haroun and the Sea of Stories* a novel for children or a novel for adults?**

The novel functions on two levels. On the first level, it is a novel for children. Its main character is a young boy. The action and adventure of the story appeal to a younger audience. The unique use of language adds playfulness to the text that appeals to a childlike imagination. On another level, the themes of the novel are meant to be understood by adults. Political, social, and artistic commentary is used in the novel's allusions and symbolism. In this way, Rushdie means to tell a tale that can be enjoyed and understood by a wide audience.

9. **Although *Haroun and the Sea of Stories* is a written novel, oral tradition plays a large role for many of the characters. Discuss what this means**

for the novel's narrative.

The oral tradition of storytelling and the orality of the stories within the novel represent an important tradition in Eastern narrative traditions. The earliest stories, those represented as pure in the Sea of Stories, were not written but were spoken by figures such as Rashid Khalifa. Rashid, therefore, symbolizes the ancient storytellers that helped to keep tradition and culture alive through the repetition of stories. Many of these stories were also told through song and so several of the characters in the novel use music as a means of passing along information about themselves or about the meaning of their world. For instance, Mali the Gardner always illuminates some characteristic about himself through song. Likewise, the Plentimaw Fish only speak in a music-like rhyme. Their lyricism is as much about creating a world as it is about communication.

10. **Is the novel's happy ending manufactured or real?**

Rushdie ends the novel without a clear resolution of whether the story's happy ending is a good thing for its characters. Haroun is obviously glad that his mother returned and it creates a happy environment for him. However, he is also disturbed that that the happy ending is synthetic, or unreal, just as was the Khattam-Shud's poison. The real meaning of the ending, perhaps, is found in Haroun's mother's song, which symbolizes that the story never really ends. Just as her singing continues, so does the meaning and narrative of all good stories.

The Source Stories

In *Haroun and the Sea of Stories*, Salman Rushdie uses an adventure narrative to ask complex and nuanced questions on the role of story and fiction in modern culture. The novel is partly autobiographical, partly philosophical, partly theoretical, but mostly a fun adventure story that itself relies on narratives dating back to the earliest oral traditions. In the novel Haroun must travel to Kahani, an invisible moon of the earth that holds the Sea of Stories. Haroun must find a way for his father to tell stories once again. To do so, he travels to the Old Zone in the Twilight Strip of Kahani, a place in between darkness and light, to battle Khattam-Shud, the Prince of Silence.

The Old Zone is Rushdie's metaphor for the religious and spiritual traditions that provide the oldest stories in humanity. These stories were originally oral traditions that were later written down and edited into texts that some came to view as sacred. These stories became sacred because they attempted to put a narrative to the deepest seeded beliefs of humanity. In the novel, Rushdie places the Old Zone in the Twilight Strip, representing his belief that the oldest of narratives are not representations of either good or evil. Instead, these stories explain a deeper truth that cannot be understood outside of the narrative device.

In religious and cultural studies, these types of narratives are often referred to as Myths. A myth (used with a lower case m) differs from a Myth (used with an uppercase M) in that the latter is a narrative tradition that has become so enmeshed within the psychological and physical culture of a society that it becomes true in a very real sense for those that hear and live within such narratives. Sociologists of religion might make the distinction between the myths of Ancient Greece or Rome, and the Myths of modern religions such as Christianity, as an example. The Greek myths are understood as stories; narratives that help us understand a certain way of life for a particular people in a particular place. For most people, the ancient Greek myths have no bearing on the particulars of their lives. The Myths of modern religion, however, create a complex braided existence for billions of people around the world. These Myths are similar to the ancient Greek stories in that they both speak of divine beings creating the world and interacting with their creation. They differ, however, in the fact that modern societies still seek meaning and transcendence in such Myths. The modern Myths are very real for many people and, in fact, have very real impacts on how a person lives their life. As some scholars argue, this is more than a simple matter of belief; for many, the stories of religion are real in that it provides an ethical, moral, and practical basis for living in a particular environment. These are the kinds of stories that Rushdie alludes to in the Old Zone.

Some of the oldest stories still in existence are creation narratives. Two of the oldest narratives are the creation story from the book of Genesis in the Hebrew Bible and the Enuma Elish, an ancient Babylonian creation myth. Both tell a story of a divine being (in the Hebrew Bible, God is named Yahweh; in the Enuma Elish, the god is named Marduk) that creates earth out of a murky void or chaos. These stories help cultures understand the reasons for existence. In the case of the God of the Hebrew Bible, these creation stories still give important meaning to the reality of creation for millions of adherents all over the world. It is worth noting that in these creation stories, and many others, existence comes from water, just as in *Haroun and the Sea of Stories*, the creation of all story comes from a sea. Duality is often important in creation myths. In Hindu myths of creation there is a cosmogony that describes a state of void in which there is neither existence or non-existence. Often, creation is born out of these dualities of light and dark, being and non-being, and water and sky.

The heroic epic is another of the most ancient narratives that provides cultural meaning. Popular retellings of these epics date back to at least two thousand years before Christ and their origins can be found much earlier. The Greeks created the most lasting and memorable of these epics. *The Illiad* and the *The Odyssey* are the two most well known hero epics. These tell the stories of Achilles the Man of War and Odysseus the Man of Many Wiles. Achilles is a warrior who exemplifies the life of glory lived for war. Odysseus is the model of an adventurer who travels to his homeland of Ithaca to take vengeance on the suitors that try to steal his wife and his homestead. Both of these characters are not simply devices for telling a narrative, however. These heroic stories embody a culture. When a person in the ancient world heard a story such as *The Odyssey*, they were not just hearing of an adventurous man. They were also learning what it means to be a Greek person -- the values and ideologies that created an entire culture and an entire worldview.

It is the use of these stories to control and manipulate that causes their demise. This is the conclusion that Rushdie reached when his own novel, *The Satanic Verses*, a novel that deals with religion and ultimate causes, was denounced and a fatwa of death was pronounced on Rushdie by the Ayatollah Khomenei of Iran. *Haroun and the Sea of Stories* is Rushdie's attempt to regain his authorial voice by returning to the most primal traditions of creation and heroism to denounce the silence imposed upon him by a dictator.

Author of ClassicNote and Sources

Lane Davis, author of ClassicNote. Completed on February 23, 2011, copyright held by GradeSaver.

Updated and revised Bella Wang February 28, 2011. Copyright held by GradeSaver.

D.M. Fletcher, ed.. Reading Rushdie: Perspectives on the Fiction of Salman Rushdie. Amsterdam: Rodopi, 1994.

Catherine Cundy. Salman Rushdie. Manchester, U.K.: Manchester University Press, 1996.

Rajeshwar Mittapalli and Joel Kuortti, eds.. Salman Rushdie: New Critical Insights. New Delhi: Atlantic Publishers and Distributors, 2003.

Dr. Agatha Taormina. "Reading Guides: Haroun and the Sea of Stories." 2009-11-05. 2011-01-07. <http://www.nvcc.edu/home/ataormina/novels/guides/titles/haroun.htm>.

"Haroun and the Sea of Stories: A Study Guide." 2011-02-01. <http://www.leasttern.com/Haroun/haroun.htm>.

Alison Lurie. "Another Dangerous Story From Salman Rushdie." 1990-11-11. 2011-02-16. <http://www.nytimes.com/books/99/04/18/specials/rushdie-haroun.html>.

Essay: Haroun's Multicolored Backdrop

by Angela Viti Beckon
September 18, 2005

Salman Rushdie's Haroun and the Sea of Stories is in many ways a simple fairy tale about magical people in a magical land. Rushdie himself admits that he first came up with the basic idea for the novel while telling stories to his son in the bathtub, and indeed, the simple structure and plot of the novel make it an ideal children's book (Nelson). While he wrote the book ostensibly for his son (as both a child and an adult), one wonders what Rushdie's other motivations and thoughts were while writing. So many aspects of the book have direct parallels to Rushdie's own circumstances and to the world he saw around him at the time that one must look at all the complexities and not simply discount the book as children's literature. What complexities, divisions, and issues did Rushdie consider in his creation of the Haroun narrative?

One cannot deny the importance of Rushdie's own personal circumstances in the writing of Haroun and the Sea of Stories because Rushdie wrote it for such personal reasons. After Rushdie's publication of The Satanic Verses, and Ayatollah Khomeini's subsequent issuing of the fatwa calling for his death, Rushdie went into hiding in Great Britain and was unable to see his family for significant periods of time. Were it not for this inability to communicate directly with his son, very likely Rushdie would not have written this book. In very real and tangible ways, Rushdie saw and felt his work being censored at this time, and so censorship becomes a major theme in Haroun, his first post-fatwa publication. As a direct connection, the character of Khattam-Shud, the dark poisoner of the Sea of Stories, closely parallels Khomeini, who is Rushdie's own enemy of stories. In the same way Khomeini tries to maintain the one truth of his country's national and religious identity by silencing Rushdie's story, Khattam-Shud maintains control over the Chupwalas by silencing them all completely. Khattam-Shud's ultimate goal is to control all, and he says, "inside every single story, inside every Stream in the Ocean, there lies a world, a story-world, that I cannot Rule at all," so he must obliterate the source of stories, just as Khomeini would have liked to obliterate the source of The Satanic Verses (Rushdie, 161).

Khattam-Shud, like Khomeini, wishes to create a world in which there is only one truth: one right and one wrong, and stories represent a divergence from that truth. Rushdie prefers to look at the world as being dynamic and narrative, as Hassumani says, "Rushdie's...novels have always pointed to the dangers involved in buying into binary systems that simplify experience into either/or categories... Religious or political leaders who present it as a system of binaries are actively creating a myth and then selling it as 'reality'" (Hassumani, 99). Rushdie criticizes this tendency of politicians to create their own "realities" when he compares Rashid's storytelling to that of politicians, saying, "Nobody ever believed anything a politico said, even though they pretended as hard as they could that they were telling the truth...But everyone had complete faith in Rashid, because he always admitted that everything he told them was completely untrue" (Rushdie, 20). Rushdie again highlights this tendency of politicians to create their own versions of reality when Haroun and Rashid meet Snooty Buttoo. Buttoo pays for Rashid's stories, but insists on "up-beat sagas only" and says, "If you want pay, then just be gay" (Rushdie, 49). By attempting to create a falsely happy world for his constituents, Buttoo is censoring Rashid, and while Rashid feels this is wrong, he compromises his ethics and goes along with things because he needs the money. After Haroun and Rashid's adventure on Kahani, they must still return to earth and Rashid must face his obligation to tell stories for Mr. Buttoo. His words, "You'd better be good; or else" are an implied threat to the physical well being of Rashid if he does not comply with his demands (Rushdie, 205), much in the same way that writers living under restrictive governments in much of the middle east were threatened with violence if their writing in any way challenged the ruling ideology. As Rashid tells his story, the audience realizes the story's connection to their own situation of being ruled by a corrupt politician, and begins to chant, "Mister Buttoo- go for good; Mr. Buttoo-khattam-shud" (Rushdie, 206). This use of the words "khattam-shud" connect the corrupt politician to the evil character in Rashid's story, but also in this context mean literally "completely finished," and state clearly that the people of the Valley of K will no longer tolerate a leader who inhibits their free speech. They indeed drive him out of their town, leaving them "free to choose leaders they actually liked" (Rushdie, 207).

Rushdie again highlights the importance of free speech when he so strikingly contrasts the Guppies with the Chupwalas. The Guppies, perpetually full of talk, do not even understand the concept of censoring themselves based on who is around them, much less the concept of censorship of others. When discussing their course of action, Haroun says, "that sounds like mutinous talk to me," but fail to comprehend his meaning and ask, "what's a Mutinus...is it a plant?" (Rushdie, 118). In fact, Rushdie asks quite overtly through his character of Butt the Hoopoe, "what is the point of giving persons Freedom of Speech...if you then say the must not utilize same? And is not the Power of Speech the greatest Power of all?" (Rushdie, 119). Here, Rushdie is perhaps referring to and denouncing the more covert censorship of the Western world, rather than the open censorship of Khomeini's Iran. In the western world, in a way that is more like what Haroun is used to, dissenters are not silenced, but instead, people simply do not utilize their freedom of speech because they are afraid or simply apathetic. When the battle between the Guppees and Chupwalas occurs, Rushdie portrays free speech and open communication as the clear reason for the Guppee's victory. He tells us, "all those arguments and debates, all that openness, had created powerful bonds of fellowship between [the Guppees]. The Chupwalas, on the other hand, turned out to be a disunited rabble," showing that the lack of communication and trust between Chupwalas led to their quick downfall (Rushdie, 185). Indeed, he goes as far as having the Chupwalas call the Guppees "liberators." This seems a gross over simplification from which we cannot draw direct parallels to the political reality of the day. Would Iranians have felt liberated had they been freed from the rule of Khomeini? On the contrary, many Iranians hailed Khomeini for bringing back their Islamic roots and creating a cohesive national identity for Iran. Indeed, many agreed Khomeini's attempt at censoring because they, like Khomeini, saw Rushdie's Satanic Verses, as an attack on and an open rejection of Islam. Rushdie does subtly admit that not all of the Chupwalas wish to be freed from their oppression in his introduction of the suicide bomber. While in character with the children's story feel of the rest of the novel, the juggler of the bomb is in fact a reference to real life fanatics, the most publicized of which are Muslim fanatics, who willingly sacrifice their own lives in order to destroy any contradictions to their one truth.

One point which Rushdie tries to impress upon his readers is the superficiality of this idea of a single truth because it leads to artificial divisions between people who do not agree on what constitutes that one truth. As Hassumani says, "Haroun attempts to deconstruct such binary oppositions by revealing them to be cultural constructs and attempts to envision the Ocean as an alternative site of heterogeneity" (95). Rushdie explores this idea of cultural constructs in his creation of the "Invisible Wall" between Chup and Gup, and the blatantly artificial means they have for maintaining such stark division. As Butt the Hoopoe explains to Haroun, "Thanks to the genius of the Eggheads at P2C2E House, the rotation of Kahani has been brought under control. As a result the Land of Gup is bathed in Endless Sunshine, while over in Chup it's always the middle of the night" (Rushdie, 80). Because of the artificial barrier of the Invisible Wall, Guppees assume that Chupwalas are evil dark creatures without ever having met any of them. Haroun, however, admits that he thinks that, "if Guppees and Chupwalas didn't hate each other so, they might actually find each other pretty interesting" (Rushdie, 125). This situation has direct parallels in the way Rushdie viewed the real world. Being Indian and Pakistani, but having spent much of his life in Great Britain, Rushdie identifies with both the Muslim and the "Western" worlds, and sees the sometimes stark division between the two as artificial. Just in the way that the Guppees put up an invisible wall, there exists between the occidental and oriental worlds a barrier that causes one to judge the other ever without having enough information to do so.

Amidst Rushdie's vivacious fantasy world, he manages to communicate his criticism of our world's many sets of binary divisions. He wants the reader to recognize that to know what conflict is, one must understand the complexities behind it and appreciate that nothing can be definitively divided between black and white. In this way, Rushdie's fanciful narrative makes more sense of conflicts between Western and Eastern worlds than the news media, which tend to portray the world in terms of "us and them."

Essay: Haroun's Multicolored Backdrop

Quiz 1

1. **In what country is the "saddest of cities" located?**
   A. Halabay
   B. Alifbay
   C. Chilibay
   D. Surifbay

2. **Rashid is given which nickname by his enemies?**
   A. Storyteller of Glory
   B. Ocean of Notions
   C. Shah of Blah
   D. Fishy Fushy

3. **What kind of fish are found in the saddest city's sea?**
   A. snapper
   B. blahfish
   C. blowfish
   D. glumfish

4. **How many brothers and sisters does Haroun have?**
   A. one
   B. two
   C. none
   D. three

5. **From whom does Haroun hear the phrase, "What's the use of stories that aren't true?"**
   A. his father
   B. his mother
   C. Mr. Sengupta
   D. Mrs. Sengupta

6. **What time is on the clocks when Rashid smashes them in his home?**
   A. 1 o'clock
   B. 2 o'clock
   C. 11 o'clock
   D. 12 o'clock

7. **Haroun has problems focusing for more than how many seconds?**
    A. 4
    B. 11
    C. 12
    D. 18

8. **What is "pussy-collar-jee?"**
    A. a strange new fish
    B. a kind of cat
    C. a mode of transportation
    D. psychology

9. **What happens if you "rush or zoom" on the road to the Valley of K?**
    A. you get there faster
    B. you will never be late
    C. you miss the beautiful sights
    D. you meet your doom

10. **Why is the bus station so crowded?**
    A. there is an emergency
    B. not enough buses
    C. everyone is on vacation
    D. buses run very late

11. **What kind of animal does Haroun think Mr. Butt looks like?**
    A. a parrot
    B. a sea lion
    C. a bear
    D. a fish

12. **What kind of bus does Mr. Butt drive?**
    A. a fifteen passenger van
    B. a magic bus
    C. a mail coach
    D. a rocket bus

13. **What Pass must the bus go through to get to the Tunnel of I?**
    A. Pass of H
    B. Pass of K
    C. Pass of Z
    D. Pass of Nothing

14. **According to Butt, what is a slippery snake?**
    A. desire
    B. need
    C. want
    D. greed

15. **What worries Haroun as they drive towards the Valley of K?**
    A. they will be overcome with darkness
    B. they will be late
    C. they will miss their connection
    D. they will die

16. **What does the word "Kosh-Mar" mean?**
    A. beauty
    B. silence
    C. darkness
    D. nightmare

17. **What is in the air on the Dull Lake?**
    A. humidity
    B. joy
    C. smoke
    D. unhappiness

18. **What land does Haroun realize they have come to in the Valley of K?**
    A. Kosh-Mar
    B. Moody Land
    C. Silent Land
    D. Middle Earth

19. **What is the name of Buttoo's houseboat?**
   A. Turtle
   B. Khamed-Me
   C. Arabian Nights Plus One
   D. Arabian Nights Plus Two

20. **What carved wooden animal sits in the middle of Haroun's bedroom?**
   A. a snake
   B. a turtle
   C. a peacock
   D. a dove

21. **What does Haroun think the genie's head looks like when he first sees his outline?**
   A. a banana
   B. an onion
   C. a peacock
   D. a pear

22. **What color is the genie's turban?**
   A. silver
   B. purple
   C. red
   D. gold

23. **What is the genie uninstalling in Haroun's bedroom?**
   A. the Story Cable
   B. the Phone hookup
   C. the Story Book line
   D. the Story Water tap

24. **What is the Grand Comptroller's name?**
   A. the Wizard
   B. the Walrus
   C. the Egghead
   D. the Beast of the East

25. **What is a comptroller?**
    A. a manager of a system
    B. a boat captain
    C. a person who controls trains
    D. a laborer

Quiz 1 Answer Key

1. **(B)** Alifbay
2. **(C)** Shah of Blah
3. **(D)** glumfish
4. **(C)** none
5. **(C)** Mr. Sengupta
6. **(C)** 11 o'clock
7. **(B)** 11
8. **(D)** psychology
9. **(D)** you meet your doom
10. **(B)** not enough buses
11. **(A)** a parrot
12. **(C)** a mail coach
13. **(A)** Pass of H
14. **(B)** need
15. **(D)** they will die
16. **(D)** nightmare
17. **(D)** unhappiness
18. **(B)** Moody Land
19. **(C)** Arabian Nights Plus One
20. **(B)** a turtle
21. **(B)** an onion
22. **(B)** purple
23. **(D)** the Story Water tap
24. **(B)** the Walrus
25. **(A)** a manager of a system

Quiz 2

1. **According to Butt the Hoopoe, what happens to a thing once it is named?**
   A. it is forgotten
   B. it loses it's specialness
   C. it is created
   D. it becomes a part of a story

2. **What happens if one only believes in what one can see?**
   A. big trouble
   B. depression
   C. sleep
   D. no more doubt

3. **Why can't the people of earth see Kahani?**
   A. it is invisible
   B. it is too far away
   C. you must believe in it to see it
   D. it moves too fast

4. **How does Butt the Hoopoe communicate?**
   A. quietly
   B. telepathically
   C. in a whisper
   D. in a very loud voice

5. **What is the "bureaucratic shortcut" that Iff attempts to use to avoid seeing the Walrus?**
   A. drinking Wishwater
   B. speaking to Prince Bolo
   C. talking to Khattam-Shud
   D. praying to Bezaban

6. **Who does Haroun see when he wishes for his father's storytelling gifts to return?**
   A. Blabbermouth
   B. his mother
   C. Mr. Sengupta
   D. Khattam-Shud

7. **Why does Iff transport Haroun into a princess rescue story?**
    A. to cheer him up
    B. to get rid of him
    C. to show him the power of Kahani
    D. to quiet him down

8. **What kind of creature does Haroun morph into while in the princess rescue story?**
    A. a liger
    B. a tiger
    C. a spider
    D. a preying mantis

9. **All of these are nicknames for Khattam-Shud except which?**
    A. Prince of Silence
    B. Arch-Enemy of all Stories
    C. Shah of Blah
    D. Foe of Speech

10. **According to Iff, how long has it been since any Guppee has been across the Twilight Strip?**
    A. fourteen years
    B. two years
    C. generations
    D. 195 days

11. **What is Mali's official title?**
    A. Floating Gardener
    B. Twister of Stories
    C. Story Tender
    D. Story Pruner

12. **Mali tells Haroun that these kinds of stories have become nothing more than "long lists of shopping expeditions."**
    A. horror stories
    B. bedtime stories
    C. romance stories
    D. mysteries

13. **What is the meaning of "Plentimaw?"**
    A. a story that never ends
    B. it has not meaning
    C. a fish that talks too much
    D. a thing with plenty of legs

14. **What is the name for the Source of Stories?**
    A. the End Zone
    B. the Old Zone
    C. the Beautiful Zone
    D. the Dark Zone

15. **Who is the head of the Guppee army?**
    A. the Title Page
    B. Blabbermouth
    C. the Bookbinder
    D. the Page Maker

16. **Why is the Walrus named the Walrus?**
    A. he has a thin mustache
    B. he has a thick mustache
    C. he speaks in a gruff voice
    D. he has tough looking skin

17. **What kind of coats do the Eggheads wear?**
    A. leather coats
    B. lab coats
    C. fur coats
    D. waist coats

18. **The Walrus and the Eggheads are references to a song by what famous music group?**
    A. the Beatles
    B. the Monkeys
    C. the Rolling Stones
    D. Led Zeppelin

19. **The names in the novel mostly are derived from what language?**
    A. English
    B. Spanish
    C. Hindustani
    D. Arabic

20. **Where do Guppees get "tasty and wicked luxury foods?"**
    A. Mars
    B. the Old Zone
    C. the Twilight Strip
    D. earth

21. **What university did Salman Rushdie attend in England?**
    A. Durham
    B. Oxford
    C. Cambridge
    D. London School of Economics

22. **How many times will Rashid have to write "I will not spy" as a punishment?**
    A. one thousand and one
    B. three hundred and four
    C. one hundred
    D. an infinite number

23. **All of these stories appear on the Pages except which one?**
    A. Bolo and the Mermaids
    B. Bolo and Juliet
    C. Bolo the Sailor
    D. Bolo and the Forty Thieves

24. **Who was in charge of changing the names of all the stories written on the Pages?**
    A. Batcheat
    B. the Comptroller
    C. the Walrus
    D. Khattam-Shud

25. **What is a cult?**

A. a small animal
B. a fanatical religious group
C. a fan club
D. a secret society

Quiz 2 Answer Key

1. **(C)** it is created
2. **(A)** big trouble
3. **(D)** it moves too fast
4. **(B)** telepathically
5. **(A)** drinking Wishwater
6. **(B)** his mother
7. **(A)** to cheer him up
8. **(C)** a spider
9. **(C)** Shah of Blah
10. **(C)** generations
11. **(A)** Floating Gardener
12. **(C)** romance stories
13. **(C)** a fish that talks too much
14. **(B)** the Old Zone
15. **(A)** the Title Page
16. **(A)** he has a thin mustache
17. **(B)** lab coats
18. **(A)** the Beatles
19. **(C)** Hindustani
20. **(D)** earth
21. **(C)** Cambridge
22. **(A)** one thousand and one
23. **(A)** Bolo and the Mermaids
24. **(A)** Batcheat
25. **(B)** a fanatical religious group

Quiz 3

1. **What horrible sacrifice do some of the followers of Khattam-Shud make as a sacrifice?**
   A. they cut out their tongues
   B. they sew their lips together
   C. they blind themselves
   D. they eat nothing but dirt

2. **What is the name of the wall that separates Chup from Gup?**
   A. Batcheat's Wall
   B. Chattergy's Wall
   C. Bolo's Wall
   D. Rashid's Wall

3. **Why do the young people of Gup go to the Twilight Strip?**
   A. because they are tired of the light
   B. because they think it has treasure
   C. because they go insane
   D. because it is dangerous

4. **Who is Bezaban?**
   A. Khattam-Shud's master
   B. an evil spirit
   C. the leader of Gup
   D. an idol to silence

5. **What special talent does Blabbermouth posses?**
   A. the gift of gab
   B. she is very fast
   C. she can speak telepathically
   D. juggling

6. **The Ayatollah Khomeini was leader of what country until his death in 1989?**
   A. Pakistan
   B. Iran
   C. Iraq
   D. Libya

7. **Why is Haroun disappointed that Blabbermouth took away his Disconnecting Tool?**
   A. he wanted to save his father
   B. he needed it to fix the Sea of Stories
   C. he wanted to use it as a weapon
   D. he wanted to become a Water Genie

8. **Why can't the Pages simply line up by Page number?**
   A. there is too much disagreement within the ranks
   B. they are just confused
   C. they must account for chapters and volumes
   D. they cannot count

9. **As he sails to Chup, Haroun says that he has jumped "out of the frying pan and into" what?**
   A. the sea
   B. the pot
   C. the fire
   D. the cooker

10. **What cry does the army shout as they sail for Chup?**
    A. For Batcheat and the Ocean
    B. For peace and speech
    C. For Good Stories and Happy Endings
    D. For Bolo and Batcheat

11. **What is the major cause of argument amongst the Pages?**
    A. Batcheat's singing ability
    B. Bolo's hairstyle
    C. the reason for war
    D. the cause of the darkness

12. **What does General Kitab do when he hears his army arguing?**
    A. he squashes debates
    B. he encourages disagreement
    C. he punishes the traitors
    D. he ignores it

13. **What does Butt the Hoopoe call Haroun's despair upon seeing the Twilight Strip?**
    A. a Heart Shadow
    B. a Night Terror
    C. a Calm Murderer
    D. a Peace Destroyer

14. **Who is Mudra fighting when Haroun finds him?**
    A. the Guppee army
    B. his shadow
    C. the Chupwala army
    D. Khattam-Shud

15. **What color is Mudra's face painted?**
    A. red
    B. blue
    C. black
    D. green

16. **What is Abhinaya?**
    A. the Perfect Language
    B. the Gesture Language
    C. the Language of Silence
    D. the Language of Darkness

17. **Who is the only person that understands Mudra's language?**
    A. Rashid
    B. Haroun
    C. Bolo
    D. Kitab

18. **Why have the Chupwalas lost control of their speech?**
    A. they have banished it
    B. they no longer like it
    C. they have forgotten it
    D. they have not used it in so long

19. **Which character is rude to Mudra upon first meeting him?**
    A. Rashid
    B. Haroun
    C. Blabbermouth
    D. Bolo

20. **What unthinkable thing has Khattam-Shud done to his shadow?**
    A. he has named it
    B. he has killed it
    C. he has separated it from his real self
    D. he has made it grow

21. **Why is Haroun the "man for the job" of finding Khattam-Shud?**
    A. he is lucky enough to try it
    B. he is stupid enough to try it
    C. he is small enough to hide
    D. he is a slave to love

22. **Which character does not accompany Haroun to the Old Zone to find Khattam-Shud?**
    A. Butt the Hoopoe
    B. Mali the Gardner
    C. the Walrus
    D. Iff the Water Genie

23. **What do the Chupwalas use to capture Haroun and his friends?**
    A. a piercing sound
    B. a net
    C. a pit
    D. a large army

24. **Who is really at fault for the poisoning of the Sea according to Iff?**
    A. the people of Gup
    B. the people of Chup
    C. Mudra
    D. Khattam-Shud

25. **What comes out of Haroun's mouth when he tries to describe the hull of Khattam-Shud's ship?**
    A. ark ark
    B. a curse
    C. the name of his father
    D. nothing

Quiz 3 Answer Key

1. **(B)** they sew their lips together
2. **(B)** Chattergy's Wall
3. **(D)** because it is dangerous
4. **(D)** an idol to silence
5. **(D)** juggling
6. **(B)** Iran
7. **(A)** he wanted to save his father
8. **(C)** they must account for chapters and volumes
9. **(C)** the fire
10. **(A)** For Batcheat and the Ocean
11. **(C)** the reason for war
12. **(B)** he encourages disagreement
13. **(A)** a Heart Shadow
14. **(B)** his shadow
15. **(D)** green
16. **(B)** the Gesture Language
17. **(A)** Rashid
18. **(D)** they have not used it in so long
19. **(D)** Bolo
20. **(C)** he has separated it from his real self
21. **(D)** he is a slave to love
22. **(C)** the Walrus
23. **(B)** a net
24. **(A)** the people of Gup
25. **(A)** ark ark

Quiz 4

1. **What is Butt the Hoopoe's brain?**
    A. a circuit board
    B. there is no brain
    C. a black box
    D. a P2C2E

2. **What small thing does Iff slip to Haroun that ends up saving them all?**
    A. a knife
    B. Wishwater
    C. a coin
    D. a special key

3. **Where does Haroun hide his Bite-a-Lite?**
    A. behind his ear
    B. under his tongue
    C. up his nose
    D. in his pocket

4. **What fills the deck of Khattam-Shud's ship?**
    A. an army
    B. machines
    C. cauldrons
    D. generators

5. **Who does Khattam-Shud look like?**
    A. Snooty Buttoo
    B. his father
    C. Prince Bolo
    D. Mr. Sengupta

6. **How does Haroun describe the experience of meeting Khattam-Shud?**
    A. an anti-climax
    B. an important moment of choice
    C. a moment of surreal fear
    D. a terrifying experience

7. **Why is Khattam-Shud slightly blurry to Haroun?**
    A. because it is so dark
    B. because it is Khattam-Shud's shadow
    C. because Khattam-Shud is not real
    D. because Haroun is sleepy

8. **What does Khattam-Shud use to create Perpetual Darkness?**
    A. drapes
    B. duct tape
    C. darkbulbs
    D. black magic

9. **According to Khattam-Shud, the world is not for fun but for what?**
    A. managing
    B. surviving
    C. overcoming
    D. controlling

10. **What character saves the day by jamming up Khattam-Shud's machines?**
    A. Haroun
    B. Butt the Hoopoe
    C. Iff
    D. Mali

11. **At what University is Salman Rushdie the Distinguished Writer in Residence?**
    A. Harvard University
    B. Emory University
    C. University of California, Davis
    D. Southern Methodist University

12. **What is the Cultmaster using to stop the stream of stories?**
    A. a manhole cover
    B. fire
    C. a giant plug
    D. a glob of glue

13. Why does Butt the Hoopoe's brain malfunction?
    A. Khattam-Shud damages it
    B. it gets wet
    C. Haroun crosses the wires
    D. it has too many miles on it

14. What wish does Haroun use to save the day?
    A. that the Guppee army will prevail
    B. that Kahani will spin again
    C. that Blabbermouth with save the Prince
    D. that his father will rescue them

15. What is the Walrus's full name?
    A. Carlton
    B. Walt the Walrus
    C. I.M.D. Walrus
    D. T.R.T. Walrus

16. What color are the Chupwala nosewarmers?
    A. orange
    B. red
    C. blue
    D. black

17. What special talent does the Chup ambassador use to trick the Guppee leadership?
    A. dancing
    B. singing
    C. juggling
    D. gymnastics

18. Who saves Prince Bolo from being killed by a bomb?
    A. Rashid
    B. Haroun
    C. Blabbermouth
    D. Kitab

19. **What most drives the Chupwalas crazy about Princess Batcheat?**
   - A. her storytelling
   - B. her talking
   - C. her singing
   - D. her bad teeth

20. **Why do the Guppees prevail so easily over the Chupwalas?**
   - A. because of their superior weapons
   - B. because of their leadership
   - C. because of their communication
   - D. because of their strategy

21. **What position does Mudra offer Blabbermouth after the war?**
   - A. Manager of Chup
   - B. official interpreter
   - C. Chief Page
   - D. Comptroller

22. **Why won't his friends accompany Haroun to see the Walrus?**
   - A. they are frightened
   - B. they are planning a surprise
   - C. they have better things to do
   - D. they can't see the Walrus

23. **What story does Rashid tell to the Valley of K upon returning?**
   - A. Haroun and the Sea of Stories
   - B. Bolo and the Battle of Bezaban
   - C. The Adventures in the Twilight Strip
   - D. The Defeat of Khattam-Shud

24. **What does the Walrus put into the rain in the sad city?**
   - A. poison
   - B. a happy ending
   - C. a story stream
   - D. a melancholy serum

25. **What day is it when Haroun wakes up in his house?**
    A. Friday
    B. his father's birthday
    C. Independence Day
    D. his birthday

Quiz 4 Answer Key

1. **(C)** a black box
2. **(B)** Wishwater
3. **(B)** under his tongue
4. **(C)** cauldrons
5. **(D)** Mr. Sengupta
6. **(A)** an anti-climax
7. **(B)** because it is Khattam-Shud's shadow
8. **(C)** darkbulbs
9. **(D)** controlling
10. **(D)** Mali
11. **(B)** Emory University
12. **(C)** a giant plug
13. **(C)** Haroun crosses the wires
14. **(B)** that Kahani will spin again
15. **(C)** I.M.D. Walrus
16. **(D)** black
17. **(C)** juggling
18. **(C)** Blabbermouth
19. **(C)** her singing
20. **(C)** because of their communication
21. **(B)** official interpreter
22. **(B)** they are planning a surprise
23. **(A)** Haroun and the Sea of Stories
24. **(B)** a happy ending
25. **(D)** his birthday

ClassicNotes

GrΛdeSaver™

Getting you the grade since 1999™

Other ClassicNotes from GradeSaver™

1984
Absalom, Absalom
Adam Bede
The Adventures of Augie
  March
The Adventures of
  Huckleberry Finn
The Adventures of Tom
  Sawyer
The Aeneid
Agamemnon
The Age of Innocence
The Alchemist (Coelho)
The Alchemist (Jonson)
Alice in Wonderland
All My Sons
All Quiet on the Western
  Front
All the King's Men
All the Pretty Horses
Allen Ginsberg's Poetry
The Ambassadors
American Beauty
And Then There Were
  None
Angela's Ashes
Animal Farm
Anna Karenina
Anthem
Antigone
Antony and Cleopatra
Aristotle's Ethics
Aristotle's Poetics
Aristotle's Politics
As I Lay Dying
As You Like It

Astrophil and Stella
Atlas Shrugged
Atonement
The Awakening
Babbitt
The Bacchae
Bartleby the Scrivener
The Bean Trees
The Bell Jar
Beloved
Benito Cereno
Beowulf
Bhagavad-Gita
Billy Budd
Black Boy
Bleak House
Bless Me, Ultima
Blindness
The Bloody Chamber
Bluest Eye
The Bonfire of the
  Vanities
The Book of the Duchess
  and Other Poems
The Book Thief
Brave New World
Breakfast at Tiffany's
Breakfast of Champions
The Brief Wondrous Life
  of Oscar Wao
The Brothers Karamazov
The Burning Plain and
  Other Stories
A Burnt-Out Case
By Night in Chile
Call of the Wild

Candide
The Canterbury Tales
Cat on a Hot Tin Roof
Cat's Cradle
Catch-22
The Catcher in the Rye
The Caucasian Chalk
  Circle
Charlotte's Web
The Cherry Orchard
The Chocolate War
The Chosen
A Christmas Carol
Christopher Marlowe's
  Poems
Chronicle of a Death
  Foretold
Civil Disobedience
Civilization and Its
  Discontents
A Clockwork Orange
The Color of Water
The Color Purple
Comedy of Errors
Communist Manifesto
A Confederacy of
  Dunces
Confessions
Connecticut Yankee in
  King Arthur's Court
The Consolation of
  Philosophy
Coriolanus
The Count of Monte
  Cristo
The Country Wife

For our full list of over 250 Study Guides, Quizzes,
Sample College Application Essays, Literature Essays and E-texts, visit:

www.gradesaver.com

ClassicNotes

GrAdeSaver™

Getting you the grade since 1999™

Other ClassicNotes from GradeSaver™

For our full list of over 250 Study Guides, Quizzes,
Sample College Application Essays, Literature Essays and E-texts, visit:

www.gradesaver.com

ClassicNotes

GradeSaver™

Getting you the grade since 1999™

Other ClassicNotes from GradeSaver™

Inherit the Wind
An Inspector Calls
Into the Wild
Invisible Man
The Island of Dr. Moreau
Jane Eyre
Jazz
The Jew of Malta
Joseph Andrews
The Joy Luck Club
Julius Caesar
The Jungle
Jungle of Cities
Kama Sutra
Kate Chopin's Short
   Stories
Kidnapped
King Lear
The Kite Runner
Last of the Mohicans
Leaves of Grass
The Legend of Sleepy
   Hollow
Leviathan
Libation Bearers
Life is Beautiful
Life of Pi
Light In August
The Lion, the Witch and
   the Wardrobe
Little Women
Lolita
Long Day's Journey Into
   Night
Look Back in Anger
Lord Jim

Lord of the Flies
The Lord of the Rings:
   The Fellowship of the
   Ring
The Lord of the Rings:
   The Return of the
   King
The Lord of the Rings:
   The Two Towers
A Lost Lady
The Lottery and Other
   Stories
Love in the Time of
   Cholera
The Love Song of J.
   Alfred Prufrock
The Lovely Bones
Lucy
Macbeth
Madame Bovary
Maggie: A Girl of the
   Streets and Other
   Stories
Manhattan Transfer
Mankind: Medieval
   Morality Plays
Mansfield Park
The Marrow of Tradition
The Master and
   Margarita
MAUS
The Mayor of
   Casterbridge
Measure for Measure
Medea
Merchant of Venice

Metamorphoses
The Metamorphosis
Middlemarch
A Midsummer Night's
   Dream
Moby Dick
A Modest Proposal and
   Other Satires
Moll Flanders
Mother Courage and Her
   Children
Mrs. Dalloway
Much Ado About
   Nothing
My Antonia
Mythology
Native Son
Nickel and Dimed: On
   (Not) Getting By in
   America
Night
Nine Stories
No Exit
Northanger Abbey
Notes from Underground
O Pioneers
The Odyssey
Oedipus Rex or Oedipus
   the King
Of Mice and Men
The Old Man and the Sea
Oliver Twist
On Liberty
On the Road
One Day in the Life of
   Ivan Denisovich

For our full list of over 250 Study Guides, Quizzes,
Sample College Application Essays, Literature Essays and E-texts, visit:

www.gradesaver.com

Made in the USA
Lexington, KY
04 July 2011